Collector's Quest

The Correspondence of Henry Miller and
J. Rives Childs, 1947–1965

"Two Figures" is a reproduction of a tempera painting by Henry Miller in the Barrett Collection of the Alderman Library, University of Virginia. The original is 18 × 19½ inches and was probably done in 1941. It is inscribed, "For John Kidis, From Henry Miller."

Collector's Quest

The Correspondence of <u>Henry **Miller**</u> and
J. Rives **Childs,** 1947–1965

Edited, with an Introduction, by
Richard Clement **Wood**
Randolph-Macon College

Published for Randolph-Macon College
Ashland, Virginia
By the University Press of Virginia
Charlottesville

Editor's Note

All the available letters exchanged by Henry Miller and J. Rives Childs are published here. A few of Miller's letters seem to have been lost or mislaid. Those surviving are now in the collection at the Walter Hines Page Library at Randolph-Macon College, Ashland, Virginia. Childs's letters are taken from copies made by Childs at the time of writing. These are also now in the collection at the Page Library. A few apparent gaps indicate that copies were lost or not made.

The editor has tried to preserve the texts of these letters, Miller's in particular, with all their evidence of haste. Some errors have been corrected, especially in Childs's letters, and several names, telephone numbers, and addresses have been replaced by long dashes. A couple of personal comments by Miller have been deleted. Titles have generally not been regularized, and French words have only those accents the writers gave them. Most of Miller's letters were handwritten. These are indicated by the symbol ♈ following the date.

The letters by persons other than Miller and Childs, such as those by Felix and Charles Gross, are relevant enough in their contexts to be printed where they fit chronologically. It was Charles Gross who sent to Childs the photograph of Miller and his public school class. It is included because views of Miller as a boy afford rectifying perspectives for his biography.

The editor has provided, among other briefer notes, Childs's account of his flight over the ruins of Marib in Yemen, legendarily the city of the Queen of Sheba. Another long note quotes Childs's recollection of his meeting with Miller in Nice.

In general, the notes give only the first edition or translation of a work referred to in a letter. Most of the first editions of Miller's works are now exhausted, but many of the titles are available in editions published by New Directions or Grove Press.

Appended to the letters are an article by Childs on collecting Miller and a check list of the Miller collection at the Walter Hines Page Library.

The editor cannot overstate his debt to Mr. Childs for information about the letters. Indispensable also has been the aid of Mrs. Flavia Reed Owen, head of the Walter Hines Page Library at Randolph-Macon College.

RICHARD CLEMENT WOOD

Randolph-Macon College
Ashland, Virginia
June, 1967

Contents

Introduction

In 1944 Henry Miller settled in Big Sur, California. There he was besieged by letters and visits from obscure persons who considered him a hero of dissent. These he answered or treated with characteristic sympathy while trying to maintain a heavy schedule of still financially unrewarding literary work and while continuing to expand his apparently inexhaustible energies in correspondence with old friends, publishers, booksellers, and members of his family in Brooklyn.

One of the first persons other than Miller himself to realize the immensity of his correspondence was Annette Kar Baxter of Barnard College. She received permission in 1956 to examine the Miller collection of manuscripts at the University of California at Los Angeles. There emerged for her a picture of Miller far different from that of the stereotyped sexual anarchist:

Everything testified to a major paradox in Miller; while his writings often depict him as outrageously irresponsible, the portrait that emerges from his correspondence is one of ultimate responsibility. Operating outside the mores of his time, he nonetheless placed the highest possible value on the integrity of human relationships.[1]

The correspondence between Henry Miller and J. Rives Childs shows the development of a friendship which might have been but a slight acquaintanceship if Miller had been less responsive to a collector's interest. Fascinated by Childs's scholarly pursuits and by his exotic ambassadorial posts (rather than by his ambassadorship), Miller offered

[1] *Henry Miller, Expatriate* (Pittsburgh: Pittsburgh University Press, 1961), pp. 181–82.

information about his publications without being solicited.

Mrs. Baxter has stated that Miller's need for time to write was so desperate at Big Sur during the fifties that he devised a form letter for answering persons unknown to him. In fact, the correspondence with Childs might never have been developed beyond one letter by each man if a third party, a mutual acquaintance of the two men, had not prompted Miller to recall Childs's first letter and to consider how unusual a man his Obelisk Press volumes had captivated.

It is characteristic of Childs as a letter writer that he rarely treated Miller to any account of his life as a career foreign service officer or to anecdotes about his posts. Childs was maintaining proper reticence. He ventured to record his enthusiasms for books to Miller, but Childs never forgot his chief purpose: to collect everything Miller had written, to obtain every scrap of information regarding publication and availability. The theme of the correspondence is Childs's quest for Milleriana, but its human interest – the author and the bibliophile, each with special reasons for respecting the other, reaching over the formal limits of the collector's need for information to engage one another in friendship – grows apace. The climax of the friendship comes in a meeting between Miller and Childs in the latter's apartment in Nice on Easter, 1961.

In spite of his long, eventful diplomatic career, Childs has accomplished more as a writer and collector-bibliographer than many professional historians and literary scholars. He has published nine books in English, he has material for several others in manuscript, and he has produced, in French, a monumental annotated bibliography of his collection of works by a prolific but long-neglected eighteenth-century French writer, Restif de la Bretonne.[2] Childs's vast collection of works by and about Jacques

---

[2] *Restif de la Bretonne* (Paris: Briffaut, 1949).

Casanova, including his own published studies, contains many rare items.[3] The correspondence with Miller attests to Childs's efforts to collect all of Miller's books (including French but not other translations). With the exception of the U.C.L.A. library, the Henry Miller Literary Society and its members, and the Barrett Collection in the Alderman Library of the University of Virginia, it is doubtful that as complete a collection as the one Childs has given to the Randolph-Macon College library exists anywhere else today.

Casanova, Restif, and Henry Miller may seem a curious trio of authors for a great-grandson of a famous Virginia Methodist bishop and a distinguished foreign officer to study and collect at great expense of time, money, and scholarly zeal. They are all gamy writers, unshirted chroniclers of carnal and even sordid loves; they have been expurgated (Casanova), scorned by reputable French publishers and consigned to oblivion (Restif), and banned in America (Miller). In view of their scandalous reputations, one may wonder at Childs's preoccupation with their works. I have never felt it necessary to ask Childs why these writers appealed to him. He is an omnivorous reader, a catholic reader with an appetite for classics no one ever called pornographic, and he has not the slightest interest in underground trash for itself. He has clearly shown that Casanova's love affairs have been allowed to obscure the man's historical importance as a diplomat and social observer, that Restif was a great reporter of his world, turning to record the sexual side of the Paris underworld only in the last years of his long writing life. Childs saw in Miller a contemporary Restif, a complex artist and citizen of the world who was being relegated to the role of pornographer by idle repute.

[3] Childs's Casanova collection has recently been given to the Walter Hines Page Library, Randolph-Macon College, Ashland, Va.

Actually, some resemblances to Miller may be seen in Childs. Although much less given to headlong confidences in writing than Miller, Childs expresses himself in private conversation with equal verve, candor, and warmth. Their appetites for books are alike in size and voracity.

As Childs explains in the *avant-propos* of his Restif bibliography, he had been purchasing Restif items since 1936, but the idea of obtaining a complete collection did not occur to him until 1945. By that time he had been buying Miller's work for six years. His sense of the likenesses between Restif and Miller made these writers complementary for him. Collecting Miller, Childs says in another place,[4] enhanced his study of Restif and helped to determine him to produce a systematic Restif bibliography.

Struck by a sentence in an article on American literature by Marcel Thiébaut, the editor of the *Revue de Paris,* but offended by the uncomplimentary import of it, Childs wrote first to Thiébaut and then to Miller about the article.[5] Miller responded enthusiastically, but there were no further letters for two years. It was Miller who next wrote to Childs. During this two-year period, Childs's leisure had been entirely absorbed by his work on Restif.

In January, 1950, Childs responded to Miller's unexpected note of October, 1949. (The slowness of the mails between Big Sur and Jidda must certainly have been frustrating to the enthusiastic collector whom Miller was generously offering to help.) From that date, despite the vagaries of distance and personal burdens, the correspondence gained pace, although the letters were fewer, and often longer, than they were after 1956, when, having completed his duties at Addis Ababa, Childs retired to Nice. Although they did not meet until 1961, both men

[4] "Collecting Henry Miller: or, What Miller Means to Me," *Private Library* (London), III (Oct., 1960), 34–37.

[5] "Parmi les livres," *Revue de Paris,* 53d année, No. 10 (Oct., 1946), pp. 153–56.

wrote with increasing affection, and Childs began to express some of his most personal thoughts to Miller.

The correspondence provides many fascinating asides and reminiscences, and it amply shows Miller's willingness – also evident in his correspondence with Lawrence Durrell – to serve a friend without being effusive.

The Letters

M. Marcel Thiebaut
La Revue de Paris
114 Avenue des Champs Elysees
Paris, France

Dear M. Thiebaut:

I have found your extremely penetrating analysis of
recent trends in American literature (*Parmi les livres,
Revue de Paris,* Octobre 1946) so far superior to the usual
observations of foreigners that I am moved to take issue
with you on one or two of your comments.

It has been particularly interesting to me to find in
your study the linking of the names of Restif de la Bretonne and Henry Miller. Unfortunately you do not pursue the parallel beyond its grosser appearance. Henry
Miller, of course, is a lineal descendant of Restif de la
Bretonne in the family of literature: their origins, careers,
and literary output offer an interesting basis of comparison which, it is to be hoped, will some day be undertaken
on a more extended scale. Both men were born into a
world in a profound state of political, social and economic
upheaval; both found themselves early in a state of rebellion against the societies in which they were born.
Both beat their wings by somewhat similar means against
what they regarded as the insanities of the times.

A gross injustice is done in my opinion in attributing
a pornographic purpose to the work of either of these two
writers. This has been, I am aware, the fate of Restif
which has contributed so largely to his disesteem in
France. A similar fate, I believe however, less likely to
overtake Miller. The appreciation of Restif's true value
by such great critics as Goethe, Schiller and Humboldt in

Germany, and Havelock Ellis in England has failed to break the silence of most French critics concerning Restif, although there have been signs in late years of a revaluation of Restif even in France. Contrary to the notions of most Americans, despite a license in French literature which has surpassed anything in the literature of England or the United States, the French have always shown themselves, by a strange incongruity, far more "pudibond" in their reaction to such license in literature than the English or Americans where such license is most frowned upon officially. I think the reason may be found in the greater attachment of the French to liberty. While a greater freedom of expression is permitted in France, French critics on the whole have shown themselves far more critical of this license, as expressed in the writings of Restif de la Bretonne and Henry Miller, than the Germans, the English or Americans. For these reasons I believe we may expect a fairer literary judgment of Miller to be pronounced [in the future] than Restif has as yet received inasmuch as the judgment pronounced by history upon most writers seems to be influenced primarily by the judgment formed of them in their country of origin. Among critics who count in England and America, Miller is gaining constantly more sympathetic hearing.

I think one must look upon the license of language in Restif and Miller as a means chosen by them to express their profound dissatisfaction with the world about them. Far from having a pornographic character, their language is to be regarded rather as a means of shocking an insensible world into listening to their expressions of distress at the shocking organization of society. Both Restif and Miller are profoundly humanitarian. The world to them is an insane asylum; to attract the attention of the inmates one must shock them into awareness. That at any rate is how I read Restif and Miller. To state that, "Dans le championnat international de la pornographie, il est certain qu'il (Miller) se classe bon premier" is to reveal a complete misconception of Miller. I do not believe that with your awareness, you would have made this error if you had read such works of Miller as *The Air Conditioned Nightmare, The Colossus of Maroussi, Hamlet,* or the *Cosmological Eye.* It is no fairer to Miller to judge him on the basis of certain passages in the *Tropic of Cancer* or the *Tropic of Capricorn* than it would be to judge Restif on the basis of *Anti-Justine.*[1]

You fail moreover to understand the irony of Miller, an irony in the great tradition of a Dean Swift, who was so affected by the misery prevailing in his time in Ireland that he wrote a *Modest Proposal for Preventing Children in Ireland from Being a Burden to Their Parents or Country and for Making Them Beneficial to the Public* (1729), in which he suggested that, of the 120,000 children in Ireland, 20,000 be kept for breeding purposes and the other 100,000 offered for sale for human consumption. Many of Swift's contemporaries took this seriously. Similarly, you appear to have taken seriously Miller's appeal, " 'Hommes, achetez un fusil et tuez-vous l'un l'autre.' Surtout ne travaillez pas. 'Il vaut mieux tuer les autres que gagner sa vie.' "[2]

What Miller is doing in these sentences is, after a review of the world, to sum up what he considers to be the prevailing spirit of the times. There is no doubt also the thought in the back of his mind that considering the present state of the world, mankind would do well to make a good job of it, as far as he is concerned. To infer, however, that this is his own philosophy of life is about as wide of the mark in an appreciation of his thinking, as to ascribe the acceptance of cannibalism to Swift.

I would not have taken issue with you, as I have done, had I not found your general thesis of recent trends in American literature of such great worth that it appeared a pity to me for it to be in any way vitiated by a misconception of Miller's worth. I have felt, however, all the more disposed to seek to correct a few departures from

J. R. C. to Marcel Thiébaut, May 2, 1947   5

an essay which reveals an exceptional appreciation of the literature of my Country.

Sincerely yours,
J. Rives Childs

[1] *The Air-conditioned Nightmare* ([New York]: New Directions, 1945); *The Colossus of Maroussi* (San Francisco: Colt Press, [1941]); *Hamlet* (with Michael Fraenkel), [Vol. I] ([Santurce, Puerto Rico]: Carrefour, [1939]), [Vol. II] (New York: Carrefour, [1941]); *The Cosmological Eye* ([Norfolk, Conn.]: New Directions, [1939]); *Tropic of Cancer* (Paris: Obelisk Press, 1934); *Tropic of Capricorn* (Paris: Obelisk Press, [1939]). Editions of *Anti-Justine* are described on pp. 338–42 in Childs's Restif bibliography.

[2] Childs refers to a passage in *Murder the Murderer* [Big Sur, [Calif.]: [Bern Porter], 1944). Thiebaut added, "Pour l'immédiat, il est partisan du massacre général." "Surtout ne travaillez pas" is also Thiebaut's sentence.

J. R. C. to Marcel Thiébaut, May 2, 1947

2   *Paris; July 7, 1947*

Cher Monsieur:

Je vous remercie vivement de votre lettre qui m'a
beaucoup intéressé. Je suis convaincu que votre appré-
ciation sur Miller est tout à fait juste et il est probable-
ment excessif de le juger d'après ses deux TROPIQUES.
Il n'en reste pas moins que dans ces deux livres il a bravé
la pudeur avec une intrépidité exceptionnelle. Person-
nellement cela ne me gêne pas mais je crois que la vul-
garisation de ces ouvrages n'est pas sans inconvénient.

En vous remerciant encore de votre lettre, je vous prie
d'agréer, cher Monsieur, l'expression de mes sentiments
bien dévoués.

Le Directeur,
Marcel Thiébaut

Monsieur J. RIVES CHILDS

Dear Mr. Childs,

   To receive a letter from Saudi Arabia concerning my
spiritual lineage with Restif de la Bretonne was an event.
To begin with, I must confess I have never read R. de
la B. I used to hear about his life and work at length
from an astrologer friend of mine in Paris, a Cuban named
Eduardo Sanchez, but I always had the feeling I would
be bored if I tried reading him. Now I am genuinely interested and will make the effort – thank you!

   There is one little brochure of mine you may not have
read – though it was translated into French and appeared
in one of the current revues – "Obscenity and the Law
of Reflection."[1] You ought to know it. What you say in
this connection (anent pornography) is true, but I went
on from there to make more significant reflections, at
least so I think.

   It is always warming to see some unknown person
taking up one's defense; it happens to me frequently, to
be sure, but I never fail to be thrilled. I do wonder,
though, if it was not a wasted effort. Who reads "La Revue de Paris" to-day? I receive nearly all the clippings
about myself, thanks to my Paris publisher, but I must
have missed Thiebaut's. To tell you the truth, I enjoy
reading these clippings largely for the perspective I get
on other writers. Besides, I read as much or more in
French as or than in English. It may also interest you to
know that in a new book coming out next month (called
"Remember to Remember," a sequel to the "Nightmare")
there is a chapter by the same title in which I pay a
lengthy tribute once again to France – 120 odd pages of
it! This represents a big slice of my book on America,
but is just as it should be because on that hallucinating
trip about the country I was more in France than in
America. I carry France about with me wherever I go.

Curious that you mentioned Swift in your letter to Thiebaut. I had just reread, after many many years, a child's version of Gulliver's Travels. What I never read are the Letters to Stella. I must soon now.

Do let me know when and where your book on R. de la B. comes out – I shall want to read it. I am much interested in Rimbaud. In fact, I began a long study, wrote two good-sized sections, and then shelved it as I am unable to give any continuous time to my work now. The first section appeared in New Directions Annual No. 9 – this year.[2] But it is with Rimbaud that I find the most amazing affinities. Also, oddly enough, with Herman Hesse, who won the Nobel Prize this year. I recommend to your attention an autobiographical account he wrote for "Horizon" (London) in the Sept. 1946 issue. It was like reading an account of my own life, making certain transpositions of course. Have just reread the last pages of his "Death and the Lover" (published by Jarrold years ago, London).[3]

Well sir, I must quit. Thank you ever so much for taking the trouble to write me as you did. I hope I've addressed this letter correctly – your handwriting is difficult sometimes. I read "American *Minister*" – yes? When I saw Jidda I immediately thought of Aden and of all that Rimbaud suffered there. Is there any connection, I wonder?

Most sincerely yours,
Henry Miller

P.S. And do you have "The World of Sex"?[4]

[1] The brochure was published by Oscar Baradinsky at the Alicat Bookshop, Yonkers, N.Y., 1945, and was reprinted in *Remember to Remember* ([New York]: New Directions, [1947]). The essay appeared also in *Now* (London; exact date not available, between 1943 and 1947) and *Tricolor* (New York), Vol. II (Feb., 1945).

[2] Part One was originally titled "When Do Angels Cease to Resemble Themselves? A Study of Rimbaud" and was published in

New Directions ([Norfolk, Conn.]), Vol. IX (1946). "Rimbaud, Part Two" was published in *New Directions in Prose and Poetry* ([New York]), Vol. XI (1949). The two parts were joined in a French edition translated by F. Roger-Cornaz and published by Mermod in Lausanne in 1952. The complete English edition was published by New Directions in 1956 and by Neville Spearman in London in the same year as *The Time of the Assassins.*

[3] *Narziss und Goldmund* (Berlin: S. Fischer, 1930); translated by Geoffrey Dunlop as *Death and the Lover* and published by Jarrolds in London in 1932.

[4] First published in 1940 by Ben Abramson of the Argus Book Shop, Chicago, in an edition limited to 250 copies.

Dear Mr. Childs –

Just had letter from Eleanor Howard telling of your recent visit.[1] She hopes we meet one day. Yes – but how, where?

You wrote once of certain analogies to Restif de la Bretonne. Thought I ought to tell you of (my) little book on Rimbaud, due out soon, in French – Mermod, Lausanne, éditeur. Wonder what you will say.

Do hope to see your "opus" when it comes out.

In haste,
Henry Miller

---

[1] Eleanor Howard is the wife of George Howard, a friend of both Miller and Childs. See Letter 12.

Dear Mr. Miller:

I was delighted to have your letter of October 1949.

I visited the Howards while in the United States and we talked much of you. I wish I could have gotten to Big Sur but I am afraid you have so many curious visitors who must worry the life out of you that I doubt if you are disappointed in having the number reduced.

I have been reading your Rosy Crucifixion and I like parts of it immensely.[1] I wonder when you wrote it. I regretted most of all the absence of an introduction which would have told us a little about when the book was written and where. It is not difficult to determine when reading the Tropics that they were written under the spell of a French atmosphere. I think your description of the telegraph company one of the finest things in modern American literature.[2] The best proof of this is I never tire of re-reading it.

I shall certainly send for your book on Rimbaud. However I am ashamed to say that I am as ignorant of him as you confess to be of Restif. I shall see that a copy of my book on Restif is sent you. I know of no other author who bears such a resemblance to you. Restif, although born in the 18th century was remarkably modern in his outlook and in his work. I am sure you would like *Monsieur Nicolas* and the *Nuits de Paris*.[3] I wonder if you are finding peace in California and whether you are ever tempted to return to France.

With warm regards,

Sincerely yours,
J. Rives Childs

---

[1] Childs refers to *Sexus* (2 v.; Paris: Obelisk Press, [1949]). *The Rosy Crucifixion* consists of *Sexus*, *Plexus* (2 v.; Paris: Obelisk Press,

[1953]), and *Nexus,* Volume I (Paris: Obelisk Press, [1960]).

² *Capricorn,* pp. 19–50.

³ *Monsieur Nicolas* (1797), *Les Nuits de Paris* (1788). In his bibliography Childs describes editions of *Les Nuits* (pp. 303–7) and *Monsieur Nicolas* (pp. 330–38).

Dear Mr. Childs –

Book One (Sexus) was written (*first draft*) in N.Y.
City – 1941–2 – six months. Revised four times, here at
Big Sur, after lapse of six years. Book 2 (*Plexus*) is fin-
ished but not yet printed. Waiting on my publisher, in
Paris. Last book (Nexus) not yet begun. Period covered
is roughly last seven years in N.Y. – *before leaving* for
Europe (1923–30).

Do send me your book on Restif de la Bretonne. Very
eager to read it. Will tackle Restif shortly. Am now, between times, writing a short volume about my experience
with books – "The World of Books," which U.C.L.A.
Librarian hopes to publish.[1] Am trying to persuade him
to let me list in Index *all* the books I remember having
read. Know of no author about whom such information
is given, do you? Of course I mean to include *all* – good
and bad, and especially those from childhood and boyhood – *the best!* I shall speak, too, of the books I have
not read – as they are equally important, I find.

A fascinating task – the "list" should complement my
life story.

Good cheer!

                                                    Henry Miller

Hope this reaches you, addressed *direct.*

---

[1] This work, encouraged by Lawrence Clark Powell, former director of the U.C.L.A. Library, was published in 1952 by New Directions as *The Books in My Life.* Apparently intended as a multivol-
ume work, only one volume has appeared.

Dear Mr. Miller:

Thank you for your letter of February 3, 1950. I hope
to be able to buy *Plexus* shortly. I have just finished
Sexus. You can smell New York in it – not a suggestion of
France. It stirred me deeply none-the-less.

No, I don't know of any book giving all that a writer
has read. The nearest thing I know is *T. E. Lawrence* by
his friends which gives a list of the books in Lawrence's
library.[1] I like your idea of including the important books
you haven't read, or that you couldn't get through. I
must confess I have never been able to get through
Homer and I don't think I would ever be tempted by
Milton or Dante. My great loves are Shakespeare,
Chekhov and Restif. I have the thirteen volumes of
Chekhov's stories which I am now reading again for the
nth time. I have recently discovered Leskov. Strangely
enough I can't interest myself in rereading Dostoevsky
but I never tire of Chekhov. I read an inane review the
other day in the *New Yorker* of a book on Maupassant
in which the reviewer spoke disparagingly of Chekhov.[2]
It made me shudder at his shallowness. Maupassant will
be forgotten when Chekhov will continue to be read by
thousands.

I am sending you a copy of my Restif. It was issued in
750 copies only and more than 100 copies have already
been sold which pleasantly surprises me. I would rather
have 750 discriminating readers than ten thousand near-
illiterate ones. I think you would greatly admire Restif.
The more I read your books the more I am struck by
your spiritual kinship. I would like very much one day
to do a study of the many traits you have in common.
Almost everything Restif ever wrote is autobiographical
or is represented as such. He wrote as you with the
greatest freedom and license. You must read *Monsieur*

Nicolas. I advise you to get the Liseux or the Jonquieres edition.[3] Restif is the Henry Miller of the 18th Century.

By the way I was quoting you the other day in a talk I had with the Crown Prince.[4] I found a holograph of yours included in Miscelleanea which I bought several years ago in New York.[5] It is [a] postcard to Bern Porter in which you say: "You seem to regard a friend as one who does something *for you.* Wouldn't it be better to look upon him first and foremost as one whom *you do something for.*" I consider this your greatest epigram and I prize it above anything I have of yours and I believe I have every one of your books which is available in print.

With warm regards,

Sincerely yours,
J. Rives Childs

[1] Arnold Walter Lawrence, ed., *T. E. Lawrence, by His Friends* (Garden City, N.Y.: Doubleday, Doran, 1937). Note particularly "Books at Cloud's Hill," pp. 425–60.

[2] Alfred Kazin, review of *Maupassant: A Lion in the Path* by Francis Steegmuller, *New Yorker,* XXV (Nov. 12, 1940), 140.

[3] The Liseux edition was published in Paris in 14 volumes in 1883. The Jonquières edition, based on the Liseux, was issued in 4 volumes in Paris in 1924.

[4] Prince Saud of Saudi Arabia.

[5] *Henry Miller Miscellanea* [Berkeley, Calif.]: Bern Porter, June, 1945.

Dear Mr. Childs,

Your letter of February 17th interested me greatly.
I'm afraid you won't get Plexus very soon – the publisher hasn't yet asked me for the script, completed
months ago. He's having his troubles with Sexus, particularly the French version, just released recently.[1]

The more you speak of Restif the more eager I am to
read him. Have asked several friends abroad to send me
his M. Nicholas and Nuits de Paris. I await your book on
him feverishly. Am I right in thinking that he had many
"obscene" passages in his books? I ask, because in coming now to a section (in this new book of mine) on the
"pornographic" and "obscene" writers, I find that I can
think only of about eight or ten books in this category,
and half of them I myself would not regard as either
one or the other. In fact, I don't think I've read more
than a half dozen at most of this kind of book. Strange,
what!

Am also pleasantly surprised that you think you have
everything of mine ever printed. Are you sure? Perhaps
I can send you something you lack?

And now I come to something close to my heart. Ever
since I got your first letter, with that Arabian stamp on
the envelope, I have wondered about your life there. At
the close of the war I wrote to several editors of large
magazines, here and in England, asking if they would
give me a commission to fly (all expenses paid) to three
cities and none other in between: Timbuctoo, Mecca
and Lhassa. None consented, of course. They are the
three cities I hope to visit before I die. As for Mecca, is
it open to non-Mohammedans? The other two are now
fairly accessible to white Christians (?) I understand.
But of Mecca I know nothing. It is a place I often dream
about.

But this is what I am coming to. . . . Could you sometime send me – or rather my little girl, Valentin, now
going on five, and a very unusual little girl – something
from Arabia, something "autochthonous"? It can be just
a trifle, so long as it has the feel of the place. Some
months back I began to save the many foreign envelopes
which I receive, both for the stamps and the handwriting, to give to her one day when she grows up. Remember me in this connection, won't you? A post card now
and then, showing street scenes, would be greatly es-
teemed.

———————

Have you thought of offering your book on Restif to a
French publisher? I should think they would take to it.
I can suggest names if you know none personally.

All good wishes, and forgive me for asking you for a
little gift. Tell me what I can do for *you?*

Cordially yours,
Henry Miller

[1] Tr. Jean-Claude Lefaure (2 v.; Paris: Éditions de la Terre de
Feu, 1949). Two French editions were published simultaneously:
one was expurgated, the other unexpurgated.

H. M. to J. R. C., March 10, 1950

Dear Mr. Miller:

I was delighted to receive your letter of March
10, 1950, which only arrived a day or two ago.
If you will use my A.P.O. address: American Embassy,
A.P.O. 616, c/o Postmaster, N.Y.C., and place domestic
airmail stamps on the letter your letters will come
through to me in a very few days.

You should have my book on Restif by now, but if you
have not received it do let me know. Apparently you did
not realize it was in French and published in Paris. I
appreciate nonetheless your offer to put me in touch
with a publisher.

Restif, I think, had the same attitude toward obscenity in literature as you have. He wrote some very free
things but never offensively, except in one work which he
wrote at the end of his life when he was very hard up
and was moved by a desire to make money. The book is
Anti-Justine, which, however, actually was never published and there are only five copies known, four of
which are in the Bibliotheque Nationale.

I have made up a list of your books which I possess
which I am enclosing. I would much appreciate it if you
would indicate to me any I do not have as I would like
to order them.

I have been much interested in your desire to visit
Timbuctoo, Mecca and Lhassa. I have never been to
any one of the three but can understand your attraction
to them. Unfortunately Christians are not permitted
access to Mecca, so that is out so far as you and I both
are concerned. Of all the cities of the world I have visited
the ones which have attracted me the most are Ispahan,
San'a, Jerusalem, Cairo, Moscow, Marrakesh and
Ouarzazate, the last named being in French Morocco.[1]
For your ready identification I may say that San'a is the

capital of Yemen and has been visited by less than one hundred foreigners.

I shall be delighted to send something characteristic of Arabia to your little girl and you will receive it shortly. Meanwhile I am enclosing a couple of postcards for her, one of Mecca and the other of Petra. I will try to find some more postcards for her. I also enclose two stamps which were recently issued on the occasion of the visit of the King of Afghanistan. If you would like to have more stamps of Arabia I would be glad to send them for her.

If you have not succeeded in finding *Monsieur Nicolas* and *Nuits de Paris* before this summer I shall try to find them for you in Paris when I get there in August.

I have just received a copy of *Remember to Remember* and think it one of your finest books. I like especially the introduction. When people accuse you of obscenity they might well be referred to this book and to the lofty sentiments you have expressed in it.

It is a great pleasure to have this exchange of correspondence with you and when I can find the time I am going to write your little girl and tell her about the interesting experiences I recently had in Yemen, from which I have just returned.

With every good wish and kindest regards, believe me,

Very cordially yours,
J. Rives Childs

P.S. I enclose a review I cut recently from the Paris Edition of the New York Herald Tribune, written by George Slocumbe, which you may not have seen.[2]

---

[1] Childs says he included Ouarzazate because it was the first Berber town he had seen "with an architecture so distinct from the Arab towns of the coast."

[2] Not yet identified.

Dear Mr. Childs –

Just got yours of April 25th from Jidda. Delighted –
the girl (Valentin) too – to see the post-cards, especially
of *Mecca* – and those stamps you enclosed. Thank you!
It was my first glimpse of Mecca. More, more! (Petra
I have seen in the movies several times and friends have
been there too – I know it intuitively.)

No, your book hasn't come yet, but books travel slowly.
Surprised to learn it's in French. Did you write it in that
language, I wonder? If so, my compliments!

Your list of my books is amazingly full. You lack only a
few brochures and a book by Thoreau (Life Without
Principle) for which I wrote a Preface. Have no extra
copy of this. Try the publisher – Mr. J. Ladd Delkin –
P.O. Box 55 – Stanford, California. He's about out of
them, but if you say you are a friend and collecting every
thing, he may come across. It's a handsome little job, his
book. I send you what I have here – "Money," "Of, By
and About" and the Schatz Catalogue with my text.
There are these still lacking – "The Amazing and Invariable Beauford Delaney," "Patchen, Man of Anger and
Light" and "The Chronology & Bibliography."[1] Alicat
Book Shop, Yonkers, can get you [the] first, and maybe
also the other two. You will see their address – oh, here
it is – 287 South Broadway, Yonkers, N.Y. Oscar
Baradinsky – nice chap – is the owner.

I must say it's thrilling to know that one in your part
of the world has all these volumes. I get a kick when I
hear from remote places, remote, foreign readers – as I
frequently do. Letters from Americans (at home) bore
me. They say absolutely nothing. They irritate, in fact.

Schatz (of Palestine) is my closest friend. A wonderful
fellow. He will return to Palestine soon, he thinks. I hope
I can join him, for a visit, next year.

When you mention Ispahan (which he knows) my hair stands on end. I can almost see it! As for Yemen, yes, we have had long talks about these wonderful artistic Jews. He has painted a few – years ago.

Do continue sending post-cards & stamps, if you will be so kind. Tell me how I may reciprocate!

Sexus (*castrated French* edition) now suppressed by Minister of Interior, Paris. In San Francisco a case is coming up soon, over the importation of the "Tropics." Doubt if it will be a victory. Maybe in 2253 A.D.

No M. Nicolas or Nuits de Paris yet – but expect them soon.

Let me know if I have put enough postage on this – 6¢. Should it not be 15¢?

More anon,

Cordially,
Henry Miller

P.S. How did you ever get to know the Howards?

---

[1] *Life without Principle* (*Three Essays*) (Stanford, Calif.: James Ladd Delkin, 1946); *Money and How It Gets That Way* (Paris: Booster Publications, [1938]); *Of, by, and about Henry Miller* (Yonkers, N.Y.: Alicat Bookshop, 1947); *Bezalel Schatz* ([San Francisco: San Francisco Museum of Art, 1949]); *The Amazing and Invariable Beauford Delaney* (Yonkers, N.Y.: Alicat Bookshop, 1945); *Patchen: Man of Anger and Light* (New York: Padell, 1947); Bern Porter, *Henry Miller: A Chronology and Bibliography* ([Berkeley, Calif.: The author, 1945]). "Delaney" was reprinted in *Remember to Remember,* and the Preface to *Life without Principle,* "Money," and "Patchen" have been collected in Henry Miller, *Stand Still like the Hummingbird* [Norfolk, Conn.]: New Directions, [1962]).

H. M. to J. R. C., May 10, 1950

Dear Mr. Childs –

A few items we may have overlooked –

1. Semblance of a Devoted Past (Fragments from Letters to Emil – about painters – blk & white water color reproductions – handsome edition, large format, limited. $10.00. I have about 3 copies.)

2. My "Preface" to "*Art in Cinema*" can be had (the little book itself) from San Francisco Museum of Art – Civic Center, S.F. (about $2.00 or less, I think).

3. The Rimbaud opus – 2 sections – appeared in "New Directions" Anthologies Nos. 9 & 11. Their address now 333–6th Ave., N.Y. The French version, by Mermod, Lausanne, due out any day.

And of course – "Into the Night Life" – when you become an "Ambassador" with plenipotentiary powers.[1]

Cordially,
Henry Miller,

---

[1] *Semblance of a Devoted Past* (Berkeley, [Calif.]: Bern Porter, [1944]). Miller's Introduction to Frank Stauffacher, ed., *Art in Cinema* (San Francisco: San Francisco Museum of Art, 1947), is entitled, "The Red Herring and the Diamond-backed Terrapin." Henry Miller and Bezalel Schatz, *Into the Night Life* (Berkeley, Calif.: Henry Miller and Bezalel Schatz, 1947) is entirely printed by silk screen, and the text, taken from *Black Spring,* is in Miller's handwriting.

Dear Mr. Miller:

I much appreciated your letters of May 10 and 12, 1950 and am especially grateful to you for sending me "Money," "Of, by and about" and the Schatz catalogue. I have written to Delkin and Baradinsky.

I find I have "Semblance of a Devoted Past" but believe I neglected to include it in the list sent you. I shall order "Art in Cinema" as I have particularly enjoyed everything you have written on the cinema and share entirely your views. This reminds me I saw a wonderful French film last summer in France, *Retour a la Vie* – a masterpiece.[1] It was made up of a number of episodes. There was one you would have particularly appreciated, namely the reaction of American WAACs in Paris to a handsome French bartender assigned to their hotel. I never dreamed a foreigner could have revealed another country's national characteristics so subtly as was accomplished in this episode. It was done with the greatest delicacy and was a scream. The WAACs' reactions were different from what French WAACs would have been and I regretted there wasn't a second episode making the comparison. If you ever have a chance to see this film don't miss it.

I have written again to Paris to confirm my request that a copy of my book be sent you. I am very disappointed you have not received it as I feel sure you will be greatly interested in certain parts of it. Yes, I wrote it in French. My wife thought this was a terrific joke when I announced my intention to do so as she has a much better knowledge of French than I, being half French, but I now have the laugh on her as the book has been very well reviewed in France.

You asked me how I got to know the Howards. It is

quite a long story. I will give you now only the highspots. In 1915 I was in Colorado Springs tutoring the half-witted son of a family there and George was at Colorado College where I met him as a fraternity brother. We immediately became great friends. I next saw him in Paris after the war when I was with the peace commission. I knew Paris well and when George showed up as an officer I introduced him around. You should have George tell you sometime of some of our experiences. I can remember as if it were yesterday taking him over to a clandestine afternoon tea dance (at that time all dancing in Paris was forbidden) near the Eiffel Tower. I was very fond of dancing in those days and used to meet a lot of people who shared this pleasure. When we got to the place I found to my astonishment people there from almost every milieu of my acquaintance from the top of French society down to dancers at the Casino. George's eyes were a sight to see when I took him around and introduced him to a dozen of those present whom I knew very well. Later we had a most interesting experience in Montmartre. George met a charming girl as we were going into a night spot and they afterwards opened a clandestine nightclub and George was on his way to becoming a wealthy man when the Ministry of Interior descended on him. But I am sure you have heard all this. If you haven't you must get George to tell it. I have kept up with him ever since and last year when I was in the United States I stopped particularly at Santa Monica to spend the night with them.

I sent your daughter a couple of Hejazi spoons, which were the most representative handicraft I could find. I hope she likes them.

I hope the "Tropics" case is a victory but I share your doubts.

Yes, you put enough postage on, 6¢ for A.P.O, air mail, which reaches me very quickly.

With cordial regards,

J. Rives Childs

P.S. Where can I get "Into the Night Life"? Is this a gag, or have you really written it?

---

[1] *Retour à la vie,* produced in 1949 in France, is a film of four sketches on the return to France of prisoners of war. The directors of the four parts were Cayatte, Clouzot, Dréville, and Lampin.

J. R. C. to H. M., May 22, 1950

Dear Mr. Miller:

I have received this morning the three pamphlets you were good enough to send me and greatly appreciate your courtesy.[1] I shall read them with the greatest interest.

I was deep in your "Remember To Remember" last night and was particularly interested in your inimitable account of life in Paris with Fred.[2] You refer to your unpublished works "Quiet Days in Clichy" and "Mara-Marignan."[3] It seems to me that ___ ___ wrote me some time ago about these but I can't put my hand on his letter. I would be happy to purchase a set of the manuscript if you should by any chance have an extra copy.

I was disturbed by the fact you have not received my book and I wrote a friend in Paris to inquire of the publisher. It was as I feared. My publisher, who is a delightful person, is rather careless and he stated he had neglected to send you a copy but promised to do so at once and I hope by the time you receive this the copy will be at hand. I am enclosing some additional postcards for your daughter. I hope she has received the two little spoons I sent her.

I am leaving here for a vacation in France at the end of July. Can I do anything for you there?

With kindest regards and my reiterated thanks for your thoughtfulness in sending me the pamphlets, believe me.

Cordially yours,
J. Rives Childs

[1] The pamphlets are apparently those mentioned in Miller's letter of May 10, 1950, as being sent. Childs must have thanked Miller for them before they arrived (Letter 12).

² Fred or "Carl" (see Letter 16) is Alfred Perlès, a friend since the thirties in Paris and author of *My Friend Henry Miller* (London: Neville Spearman, 1955; New York: John Day, 1956).

³ These stories were published as *Quiet Days in Clichy* (Paris: Olympia Press, 1956).

J. R. C. to H. M., June 5, 1950

Dear Mr. Childs –

Just before your letter (5/22) arrived, saw copy of
National Geographic, giving pictures of San'a and other
places in Yemen.[1] Quite wonderful, yes! The spoons
arrived and Val was delighted with them – and thanks
you – can't write yet. Curious handiwork!

Have you not yet read Rimbaud? Aden is so near. That
was his private "hell." Then Abyssinia – coffee planta-
tions, etc. What a life! Reading the Koran to the children
there. *Et cetera.*

Did I ever send you a copy of Cossery's "Les Fainéants
dans la vallée fertile"?[2] Would like to.

No, "Into the Night Life" is not at all a joke. I have all
the copies here. We have no publisher or distributor. The
whole thing executed by us together – mainly by Schatz
– I supplied text and my handwriting of text – in all
varieties of calligraphy. The point is it costs $100.00 per
copy. "That's no joke." I'd be only too glad to send you
one if you could afford such a sum. I think it is unique –
in book production. If you did want a copy, how would
we address the package exactly – for utmost safety.
Would send it registered or insured, if possible, of course.

This in haste,

Warmly yours,
Henry Miller

Congratulate you on writing your book in French. Wish
I could do as much!

---

[1] Illustrations for H. B. Clark, "Yemen, Southern Arabia's Moun-
tain Wonderland," *National Geographic Magazine,* XCII (Nov.,
1947), 631–72.

[2] The book by Albert Cossery (Paris: Domat-Monchrestien, 1948)
was translated by W. Goyen as *The Lazy Ones* (London: Peter
Owen, 1952).

Dear Mr. Childs –

Your *enormous* book on Bretonne finally came. To look at it floors me! What a labor! And – when will I ever get time to read through to the end? You're a real "bibliographer." Were you ever a librarian? Send an announcement of the book to my friend – Dr. Lawrence C. Powell – U.C.L.A. Library – 405 Hilgard Ave. Los Angeles (24). He'll surely want one for the library.

I enclose notice of recordings – in case you have a "long-playing" apparatus.[1] The record I marked will touch you.

In haste,
Henry Miller

---

[1] Passages from *Black Spring* and *The Colossus of Maroussi* (with comment), two 33⅓ R.P.M. long-playing records, ed. Louis and Bebe Barron, were produced by Sound Portraits (New York, 1949).

Dear Mr. Childs –

Your letter of June 5th, with the marvelous post cards,
has just come. I can't thank you enough for the cards. I
feel as if I were actually there – in Mecca. I explain each
one to Valentin – later, she will come to realize for her-
self just how precious they are.

By now you'll have heard that I received your book.
I'll have to tackle it slowly – it's a big order! But I'm truly
grateful to have it.

You mention my friend Fred – or, as I call him in my
books – Carl. I've been hunting up copies of the MSS.
you ask about. I find "Mara-Marignan" but not "Quiet
Days in Clichy" – not yet, at any rate. Feel a sudden
panic about it. The original went to a Swiss chap who
was to translate it. Anyway, herewith "M. M," in which
Carl figures again – and also, because I had *two* extra
copies, one of "The Waters Reglitterized," which may be
published in Paris – in French.[1] It's impossible to put a
price on such things. Send me anything you like, as a
token. And do hold on to the "M. M." MS. It's my last
copy. The original should be with the Swiss chap – if he's
still alive.

A friend writes me that "Monsieur Nicolas" is in 6 vols.
(in English).[2] Suppose I'll never get it. But some American library may have it.

Did I ever send you the French edition of a neighbor's
(simple) story on "Big Sur" – for which I wrote a preface?[3] It may give you an idea of this country. Let me
know – I have a few copies here.

All the best meanwhile

Henry Miller

P.S. Sending (2) MSS. in separate envelope, ordinary
mail, registered.

P.S. What I *would* like from Paris, if you can find a way to get them to me, are the two French versions of my book, *Sexus*. If you could bother to call on my publisher, Maurice Girodias of Éditions du Chêne,[4] and explain the situation, I'm sure he would give you copies for me.

Incidentally, there's a de luxe illustrated edition of "Cancer" I never mention the existence of because I detest the illustrations – by Timar, I think – committed suicide recently. Published by Editions des Deux Rives or else de la Rive Gauche.[5] Girodias will know. George Howard would like this, I feel pretty certain.

---

[1] *The Waters Reglitterized* ([San Jose, Calif.]: John Kidis, 1950). There has been no French edition as yet.

[2] Published by John Rodker in London, 1930–31; this six-volume edition was edited with an Introduction by Havelock Ellis and translated by R. Crowdy Mathers.

[3] Lillian Bos Ross, *Big Sur* (Paris: Denoël, 1948). This translation of *The Stranger* was done by François Villié.

[4] Maurice Girodias is the son of Jack Kahane, founder of the Obelisk Press. Girodias changed the name of the firm to Éditions du Chêne and later to the Olympia Press.

[5] *Tropique du Cancer,* tr. Paul Rivert and illus. Timar (Paris: Éditions des Deux-Rives, 1947).

H. M. to J. R. C., June 24, 1950

Dear Mr. Miller:

Your letters of June 20th and 24th have come in quick succession and I am grateful to you for them.

However, I am aghast at the thought that you have let me have your only copy of *Mara*. You may be sure that I shall guard it preciously and will return it to you at any time you may need it. I have found ＿＿ ＿＿'s letter and you may be interested in what he writes about your typescripts:

> "Regarding Henry . . . We saw him recently on our way to San Francisco and I got from him some additional manuscripts. Do you remember the three I had in Washington? They were in a binder with "Mara-Marignan" and "Quiet Days in Clichy." You read them all there. I have since gotten hold of another copy of the manuscript and three additional pieces of the same length which I think completes it. If you want the six pieces I can send them to you . . . You have read "The French Way," "Black Mass" and "Rue de Screw." It's excellent Miller material; probably never will be published . . . I don't know of any other complete set except the one Kinsey[1] has and I helped him complete his. Let me know if you want it. It will cost you $60.00."

＿＿ speaks of six parts and when he does so I suppose he includes "Mara," "Quiet Days," "The Waters Reglitterized," "The French Way," "Black Mass," and "Rue de Screw." If it is agreeable I propose to pay you the sum ＿＿ asked which would mean $10 for each part with the understanding, however, that they are on loan to me and that you may have them back whenever you ask for them. I quoted ＿＿'s letter to reassure you that a copy of "Quiet Days" was available with him.

No, I am not a librarian but am deeply interested in

books. I have sent a notice of the Restif to Dr. Powell as you suggest.

I shall look up Girodias when I get to Paris and try to get the French texts to you. The English text of Restif is in six volumes and is expensive. I bought my set before the war for £5, but it sells now for about £10. I would recommend the four volume set published by Jonquieres with very delightful illustrations in the style of the 18th century. This should be had for about four or five thousand francs. If I run across a set I will send it to you.

I am delighted little Valentin found the postcards interesting. I obtained all of any interest whatsoever.

When you look at my Restif I suggest you read the comments under the *Paysan perverti* in the second part.[2] I think you will find especially interesting the development of him as a writer as shown in the comments under his works which, of course, are given chronologically. I dug out everything he himself had had to say about his books and brought these comments together when I listed his works. It is a book to dip in rather than to read through, that is, unless you have an abiding passion for Restif as I have.

I leave for France in two weeks and will be gone until October.

All the best, as always,

J. Rives Childs

[1] The librarian at the Institute for Sex Research, Inc., Indiana University, reports the receipt of nine purportedly Miller manuscripts as follows: in 1946, from an anonymous donor, "Cherchez la toit," "France in My Pants," and "Sous les toits de Paris"; and in 1949, from ___ ___, "Mara-Marignan Marinated," "Quiet Days at Clichy," "Black Mass," "Paris de luxe," "The French Way," and "La Rue de Screw."

[2] Childs refers to his extensive note on the composition of the *Paysan perverti*, pp. 228–39. He drew extensively upon Restif's letters for this section.

Dear Mr. Childs –

Just the day to write you a few words about your book
on Restif, the photographs, and other things.[1] When I
opened your book and saw the vast agglomeration of
data restiviennes I felt defeated. You know that at present
I am reading more than I ever did before, because of the
book I am now working on.[2] I am inundated with books
from all parts of the globe, it seems. And, not having read
a line of Restif de la Bretonne, it seemed useless to me
to wade through all these notes, these views and counter-
views, references, etc. etc. etc. Simply formidable. . . .

This morning, however, after penning a letter to my
old friend Eugene Jolas (of "Transition") whose little
book "The Language of Night" I had just re-read,[3] I took
down your tome and read the Preface and the Avant-
Propos. At once I saw why you insisted on my becoming
acquainted with this author. That, at various times, you
have linked my name with his, now of course appears
more than ever flattering. When, however, I came to your
words on page 13, wherein you state why he is "un
caractère sympathique," I realized immediately that he
is a blood-brother. All that he was and sought to be – how
shall I put it without seeming egotistical? – well, that is
how I (secretly) regard myself. I don't mean to say that
I *am* to be compared with him, but the tendencies, the
trends, the aims, the quests, the preoccupations, all are
dreadfully and intimately familiar. I feel I can avow this
to you naturally and frankly.

But to come to *you*, your part in all this . . . I must
say that I do not see how any one, not giving his *whole*
time to such an endeavor, could have accomplished
what you did. It is simply staggering, your labors. There
is one man in France to-day who would appreciate what

you have done, I do believe, and that is my friend Blaise Cendrars, about whom I have written at some length in this present book.[4] He once undertook something similar in connection with the life of our own John Paul Jones: his researches and explorations constitute a book in themselves. Incidentally, I believe he dropped the idea altogether, though with Cendrars one can never say anything with certainty. At ninety-five he may come forth with the promised work! I know too that André Breton was vastly interested in Restif.[5] No doubt he has already discovered your book.

His uniqueness, his originality, emphasized by you and by Pasteur Valléry-Radot[6] – especially that last paragraph of the latter's – impress me. As also your fleeting remarks – why did you not expatiate more, I wonder, not on this alone but on all his phases – on the "pornographic" or obscene elements in his work. (I suppose you are certain of what you say, in this connection, that the eruption of the sexual element late in his career was a form of compensation?) I ask only because, with most "great" artists, as they advance in age, their work becomes more simplified – and more daring – that is to say, more absolutely in accord with their real, inner nature, until finally it is a veritable blaze of light, the soul aflame, so to speak.

And your footnote on his American vision – that reminds me vividly of de Sade who was also prophetic in this respect.

I would indeed like to know what he said of Jeanne d'Arc. Just two nights ago I finished a book on a character the like of which I never heard of nor expect to hear of again – Gilles de Rais. Who was one of Joan's chief "lieutenants." The sort of individual which only the Middle Ages could have thrown up. The book I speak of was called "Gilles de Rais" (Et son Temps) by Georges Meunier, Nouvelles Editions, Latines, 1, rue Palatine, Paris (6) – 1949. You may wish to read it, though how you can read anything else but Restif and his commentators is beyond me!

I have been studying your physiognomy for some time. You remind me of some one I know but can't recall who it is. What *is* strange, disconcerting, is to see those other "types" about you. They belong in their setting – you don't. In the one of you seated with hand to chin I see great sensitivity. Sensuous sensitivity. And with this a peculiar combination of the executive and the judicial. I can see a little more – the presence of an intelligence capable of absorbing, analyzing and evaluating *anything*. (I wonder how right I am in these quick observations?)

Photos of men I like or admire mean a great deal to me. I am never without a few on my walls. At present it is – Grock (the clown) Cendrars and Beauford Delaney (the Negro painter) – all tremendously assertive (photogenetically)! I used to have always on the wall – Keyserling (in his Mongol aspect), Krishnamurti, Romain Rolland (chauve souris!). Now, over the door of the house, as a "benediction" I have that unknown Chinese sage whose face you may recall in a photo I think I sent you once. This "unknown" is closer to me than all the known ones – and he radiates light!

I come back to the post-cards. Looking at them, as I do now and again, gives me weird, almost hallucinating, feelings. I cannot believe I am looking into Mecca. I am amazed that the Moslems permit this much of a view. But what architecture! Sometimes reminiscent of Roman ruins, sometimes of ghetto scenes from New York. *Yemen* had shots which reminded me even of Park Avenue – though it would be hard to explain to you just why. But there is a curious "suspended interval," for want of a better expression, in these architectural impressions. Something hangs over from Greco-Roman times and impinges on modern times, with faint reverberations of the General Grant tombstone style of Brooklyn–New York architecture. The best I can do, suggestively, at the mo-

H. M. to J. R. C., July 14, 1950

ment. But haunting, haunting. Some day I may write about it better. I am on the track of something and it is connected with the "déjà vu" theme.

But enough! Warm wishes always.

Henry Miller

[1] Childs cannot now recall what the photographs were. They may have included photographs of him which Miller had requested.

[2] *The Books in My Life.*

[3] The Hague: The Servire Press, 1932. Jolas was the editor of *Transition* from 1927 until 1938.

[4] *The Books in My Life,* chap. iii, pp. 58–80. For a recent biographical and critical study of Cendrars and his work see the Introduction by Walter Albert and the Preface by Henry Miller in *Selected Writings of Blaise Cendrars* (New York: New Directions, 1966). Cendrars died January 21, 1961.

[5] Breton, poet, essayist, and critic, was a founder of the surrealist movement.

[6] Louis Pasteur Valléry-Radot, French physician, writer, and member of the French Academy, the grandson of Louis Pasteur. He wrote the Preface to Childs's Restif bibliography.

Dear Mr. Childs –

Your letter of July 6th, quoting from ____ ____'s letter
– what a coincidence! Just a very few days ago I wrote a
Hollywood bookseller (Lee Treeson) who tried to sell
three of these pieces(*) to a friend of mine, another bookseller, in Sacramento, that they were definitely not mine.
He had bought them of a friend of a friend of mine –
names not mentioned. Said I had offered them for sale
when hard up – in New York. The whole works – all in
typescript – had been given the title – "Opus
Pisorium"(?). The titles of the three you mention *I* could
never have invented! They are completely out of my
"line." I abhor erotica – this sort – "smut for smut's sake"
– as I suppose them to be. Now, it is possible "they" invented these titles too – perhaps for pieces I *have* written
– but I doubt it strongly. I know every thing I have
written – and I know I never sold any one, or gave any
one, typescripts of unpublished material.

As for ____ – now it becomes truly delicate and still
more puzzling! I am quite certain I did *not* give ____ any
MSS. when he was here a year or so ago. I do not even
recall giving him "Mara" or "Quiet Days." I have a suspi-
cion he got them from the bookseller Ben Abramson (a
good friend of his), of the Argus Book Shop.[1] I gave Ben
these two scripts to publish privately – several years ago.
He never did. He never returned the scripts either,
though I have asked for them repeatedly. And to think
poor Dr. Kinsey believes all this crap to be mine!

What confirms my convictions is this. In Hollywood
five or six years [ago,] I was shown, by a book dealer,
some typescripts he had bought to which my name was
signed. He paid a good price for them. When I told him
they were not mine, he seemed incredulous. I have a
feeling they are the same scripts. Unfortunately, I no

longer remember the titles of these. I read a few pages of each and was amazed that any one could have believed them to be mine. I am amazed that ＿＿ should also think them mine – "excellent Miller material." In another way I am not – because ＿＿ is interested almost solely in the "erotic" element. And then the price! That amazes me still more. If I had "given" them to him, as he says, was it to sell them? It's incomprehensible.

I *have* sold MSS. – hand & typewritten – *after* a work was published – for the value of the "corrections" and "revisions." I never sold even the slightest thing for *ten* dollars. Absurd. I was reluctant to put a price on yours, first because I felt indebted to you, second, because what I would like to receive for such things I never have the nerve to ask.

But – to be absolutely sure of what I say – mail these three scripts to me, if you like. I will tell you the truth on reading them. But before doing so, compare with my other writings! Perhaps it will then be unnecessary. I don't have a left and a right hand – in writing, as you probably know. If I had, I would have made money writing for the paying magazines. If this letter is a bit tart, believe me, there is no animus directed towards *you*. Your check is entirely satisfactory to me, and accepted graciously. I'm glad you had the impulse to write me as you did. And it was kind of you to offer to lend me the "Mara" (to retype) should the original be lost. I'll never get the ones that went to Abramson, I realize that. He's probably waiting for me to die.

If you feel inclined, try to look up Blaise Cendrars – now living at 100 Blvd. de Port-Royal, Paris. I think you will find him a rich character – and undoubtedly an admirer of Restif. Phone or write him first, though! He's touchy.

I'm going to look up the reference you give to-night. Wrote you a few days ago – about the book – after a first dip into it.

About ＿＿ – use your discretion! I wouldn't want to

hurt his feelings. But there's something damned *"louche"* about the whole business.

Warmly yours,
Henry Miller

P.S. Oh yes, if you are floating about in Paris, have a look in on Pierre Laleure, a good bookseller friend – fond of Montaigne. He lives on avenue Hoche but his shop is elsewhere. See the Bottin!

P.S. If you have an address when abroad, let me know – may want to write you. If possible, try to get some inkling of *who* or *what* is behind the current police attacks on my books, yes? I have a notion *our compatriots* are back of it.

---

* "The French Way," "Black Mass" and "Rue de Screw." Never even thought of writing about a black mass–beyond me! Rue de Screw–an insult to the French! It makes me furious, these titles. [Miller's note.]

[1] In 1939 Childs visited Abramson's New York bookstore and purchased some unbanned Miller books. At that time Abramson and Frances Steloff of the Gotham Book Mart were the only dealers in New York trying to carry them. Later Abramson opened the Argus Book Shop in Chicago and in 1941 met Miller and sought to become a clearing house for his books and manuscripts.

Dear Mr. Childs –

In my last there was a complete oversight. I suggested you compare those (3) pieces with the "phony" titles with my other writings, forgetting that ___ ___ had them, *not you!*

I enclose clipping just sent me by a fan.[1] Jack Kahane had the idea in 1937 or '38 of bringing out, in English, the "120 Days" of de Sade. Wonder if Girodias is serious about Bretonne, etc.?[2]

Letter from his secretary yesterday gives me the following information:

". . . Pour "Sexus" la Justice a été dénichée une ancienne loi de 1881 qui n'a rien à voir avec votre ouvrage. Cette loi permettait au Ministre de l'Intérieur d'interdire la circulation en France de "tous écrits de provenance étrangère" et avait surtout un but politique. On a donc détourné l'objet de la loi en signant l'arrêté du 6 Mars 1950. M. Girodias a du reste décidé d'intenter une action devant le Conseil d'Etat demandant d'abroger cet arrêté ministériel. Mais cette action sera certainement longue."

The first edition of "Sexus" is about exhausted. A new, cheaper edition, in one volume, on "Bible paper" (?) is in preparation, she adds.

You might return the clipping any time at your convenience.

Cordially yours,
Henry Miller

P.S. In Paris you should be able to see the "Night Life" book at Brentano's. See Mr. Davis there – an old friend.

---

[1] The clipping has not been identified.
[2] Translations of de Sade and of *Anti-Justine* of Restif de la Bretonne were subsequently published by the Olympia Press.

Dear Mr. Miller:

I feel very badly indeed about not having replied
sooner to your very much appreciated letter of July 14th
commenting on my Restif book. Your letters of July 21st
and 25th, forwarded from Jidda, reached me here today
and reminded me of my omission.

The fact is I left Jidda on July 23rd with an intestinal
disorder which has plagued me for some time: in fact it
has been the bane of my existence for years. If you knew
me you would not say I was lacking in guts figuratively
but I have none literally. I went to Austria for a rest
where life is incredibly cheap but rather dull. Then to
spend three days in Venice doing nothing but sitting in
St. Mark's Square and admiring one of the most beautiful
spots on earth. Then two weeks ago I came here with
my wife where I have been coming for the last four years
in an effort to obtain at least partial relief. I love Vichy
and it grows dearer to me every year. We stay at a
modest hotel because we knew the proprietor in Morocco during the war and also because I hate luxury
hotels which are mostly frequented by gangsters and
gangsters' molls and by shady uninteresting people. The
food is out of this world and we pay for both of us for
everything 3,000 francs a day or about $4.25 each a day.
We have been seeing some amusing French shows and
movies, including RETOUR A LA VIE, about which I
have written you which I saw for the second time and
was more impressed the second time than the first.
There are some sublime passages in it. The movie consists
of five episodes concerned with the post-war period. The
first episode might be called "Human greed." It is about
a family which forged the name of a sister to a property
document while she was in a German concentration camp
from which she was never expected to return. She did
return and you see her lying emaciated on a bed while

the members of her family go in one by one to persuade her to legalize what they have done. The punch about this episode is her concern for her dog! What happened to it? That is all she cares about.

The second episode is laid in an American Wac hotel in Paris. An old bartender gives the job of night bartender to one of his copains who returns from the war. There is a rule in the Wac ranks that no man can be entertained in the hotel after midnight and then only in the public rooms. The girls don't notice the handsome new bartender until one night after all the American officers have had to depart and then one by one they retire to their rooms and telephone the bartender to bring them drinks. In the end however their innate prudery brings them back to a sense of the strict discipline which they have been taught to maintain and they dismiss the bartender. I consider this a masterpiece of psychology on the part of the French director. Can you imagine French Wacs behaving in this way. The third episode is one in which the French have a good laugh at themselves. The Mayor is pacing the floor reading a prepared script of a typically pompous speech welcoming returning French prisoners. The authorities have selected one particularly meritorious case to receive the tribute of the Mayor but in the middle of the speech a functionary steps up to tell the Mayor that M. Martin to whom he is making it is the wrong man. However the Mayor decides to go on and Martin receives a statuette which is subsequently broken over his head by a crowd of American and British soldiers in a bar. Martin goes home to find that his apartment has been requisitioned by a displaced family and books which he loved are being used as building blocks by the children of the family. However his old dogs recognize him and he is happy to have a room given him in his old apartment and to find one or two of his old suits which he had left behind. The fourth episode is portrayed by that great French actor, Louis Jouvet. The scene is in a boarding house. A member of the German Gestapo has escaped from the French police and seeks refuge in Jouvet's room. The German is a former professor and Jouvet hides him because he wants to find out what made a man of the German's intellectual background torture and kill his fellowmen. In the end when they are about to enter Jouvet's room to lead the GERMAN OFF Jouvet administers poison to him so he may not be subject to the prison treatment he inflicted upon others. The last episode is the story of a Frenchman who returns to a French village with a German wife. Everyone boycotts them and makes the German girl's life so miserable that she jumps into a pond. The officials in the village who have been most vehement against the girl jump in the pond to save her.

This is a very poor and inadequate description of one of the greatest films I have ever seen. Hollywood has not sufficient imagination to produce such a film. It will certainly be shown eventually in America but it is so subtle in many places and the American people's minds have been so debased by Hollywood that only a rare few will appreciate it.

Now to reply to your letters and first of all that of July 14th. No, I am not at all certain that the eruption of the sexual element late in the career of Restif was a form of compensation. This was a mere supposition on my part and I may be entirely wrong. Restif was actually always preoccupied with the sexual element and his earliest literary compositions were erotic verses.

Restif's remarks on Joan of Arc are to be found in his *Prevention Nationale.*[1] Unfortunately my Restif books are all in cases at a flat we have found in Nice or I would copy the reference out and send it to you. In this connection I think so often of one of Gautier's essays where he wrote of one of his friends who had never accomplished anything in life but in Gautier's opinion had justified his existence by his love and appreciation of Shakespeare. When the friend died this was the epitaph chosen for his grave: "He loved Shakespeare." I read this perhaps thirty years ago but I still remember the thrill this little essay gave me.[2]

I am devoted to the French and love even their weaknesses. I don't believe I could find genuine happiness anywhere else but in France. I intend to spend my last years here, unless the Russians interfere.

I am glad you liked the postcards. Your comments on Yemen reminding you of Park Avenue were exceedingly apropos. The high buildings of Sana from a distance give that old city a strangely modern appearance. I must send you some photos I took in Yemen when I get settled. This spring I flew over the forbidden city of Marib, ancient capital of the Queen of Saba or Sheba and took the first photographs ever taken of that mysterious settlement which lies just on the edge of the great Arabian desert.[3]

I think you are absolutely correct in your assumption that _____ probably obtained his MSS from Abramson. I have had the same experience with the latter that you have had. I left books with him to be sold for which he has never given me an accounting and I left a Mss of a book I wrote on Tangier (which I consider one of the best things I have ever written)[4] but he has never returned it despite my repeated requests and now leaves my letters unanswered. . . . _____ told me last year he had obtained a settlement from him only after threatening him with a suit. I have recently done the same in an effort to get my Mss back. So far I have only threatened and hoped that this would bring results but it hasn't.

I am returning the clipping you so kindly sent. I must drop in and see Girodias when in Paris and what his plans are about Restif. Very interesting. He doesn't seem to realize "Monsieur Nicolas" has been translated into English. Even Somerset Maugham was not aware of this when we spoke of Restif. I told Maugham I had been disappointed he had not mentioned Restif in his "Notebooks" which I had enjoyed reading immensely.[5] His reply was: "He was a bawdy writer of the 18th century, wasn't he?" I tried to convince him he was something more than a "bawdy" writer but Restif has gained that reputation just as you have from people who either haven't read you or who are incapable of understanding what they read. As I have said so often you are Restif's spiritual descendant and you personify for us all that he did for his century. If I believed in reincarnation I would suspect you were a reincarnation of Restif. I must do a comparative study of you two one day.

You inquired about my plans. We leave here on the 17th for the Balearic Islands for a few days as my wife doesn't like Paris and wishes to look around and decide whether we are to make our principal home there when I retire. I shall be in Nice about the 26th and leave for Paris on Oct. 8th (address: American Embassy, Paris, Visitor's Mail Room). I sail on the Liberté on the 18th for New York and will be in Washington for about a month (address in Washington: Cosmos Club).

I expect to be back in France in December and will probably sail for Djibouti at the end of that month as I am probably going as ambassador to Ethiopia, the land of Rimbaud, but for the moment this is all confidential.

I have misplaced the name of the person you wanted me to see at the Obelisk Press about French editions of your works. I shall try to raise the question with Girodias but if you will send me the name of the Frenchman you mentioned I shall be glad to see him.

All the best to you and my renewed excuses for not writing sooner.

Ever cordially yours,
J. Rives Childs

---

[1] A five-act play which was published in 1784. See Childs, *Restif,* pp. 284–85.

[2] As Théophile Gautier tells the story in *Histoire du romantisme* (Paris: Charpentier, 1874), pp, 34–43, "Jules Vabre loved Shakespeare, but with an excessive love. . . . He thought of him in the day and dreamed of him at night. . . . Vabre would willingly have

stopped people in the street to ask of them: 'Have you read Shakespeare?' . . . If he is no longer living and has a tombstone somewhere, one can read on the stone as his only epitaph: He Loved Shakespeare." Childs tells the story several times.

[3] Childs may have been wrong in believing that the photographs referred to were the first ever made. André Malraux says that he and a companion flew over Marib and took pictures in 1934 (Malraux, *Antimémoires* [Paris: Gallimard, 1967], pp. 83 ff.). His claim has, however, been disputed. In any case Childs's flight was not without certain dramatic aspects. While on an ambassadorial mission within the borders of Yemen, Childs persuaded his pilot to fly over a section of the desert where Marib was thought to be located. Just before discovery of the site the pilot announced that there was only enough fuel to reach the appointed destination. Nevertheless he went on and circled the city once while the photographer aboard took pictures. The plane was obliged to land for refueling on a British airstrip on Kamaran Island. Childs was five hours late for his diplomatic appointment and is sure that the Yemeni officials knew why he was late and where he had been.

[4] The manuscript was a spy thriller entitled "Satan's Rendezvous," the scene of which was Tangier.

[5] *A Writer's Notebook* (London: Heinemann, 1949).

Dear Mr. Childs,

It was indeed generous of you to write me at such
length, in view of the fact that you are taking a cure. I
enjoyed all you wrote about the French movie, which
will doubtless be shown here soon, in Carmel – we do get
foreign films here.

I do keep my correspondence and, in returning yours
as you request, hope you will let me have it back later.
The news of Ethiopia is excellent, though Djibouti is a
"hell-hole," is it not? Rimbaud wrote frightful descriptions
about the "oven" of Aden. I so much wonder what stories
you will hear about him when you get there. He was a
very great linguist, I suppose you know, and read the
Koran to the native children, among other things.

Strange, how long it takes for one of Restif's books to
reach me. Every letter you write me makes me more
eager to read him. I forgot about the preface to Rage de
Vivre. It was originally a letter, not intended as a preface,
but Duhamel wanted it as a preface. The English title
is "Really the Blues," without my preface, naturally.[1]
Another preface I had forgotten just turned up, in an
English edition of "The Power Within Us," by Haniel
Long; Henry Drummond, London, publisher – don't have
address at this moment. A very good preface, I think.
Did not appear in the American edition. Nor did I ever
see a copy of the English edition until the other day –
published about four or five years ago.[2] There's another
due out, soon, in French – for Wallace Fowlie's book, The
Clown's Grail – Le Graal du clown.[3] Forget publisher;
but if you want the book, which I thought superb, write
to Fowlie c/o Bennington College, Bennington, Vermont.
I also wrote one for Alfred Perles' "The Renegade" (England)[4] and for James Hanley's "No Directions" (England

– also French).[5] There are probably more I don't recall now.

Do you keep things I've written for magazines too? Fragments of Plexus have appeared in two World Review issues and one from my book about books is coming out now in "Survival," N.Y.[6] But I can't keep up with all this data. The best, for such information, is to write the Director of the U.C.L.A. Library, 405 Hilgard Avenue, Los Angeles (24). He tries to collect everything that appears under my name – and has indeed a wonderful collection.

I hope this letter, with your own included, reaches you in Paris. The French author I mentioned was Blaise Cendrars, *now* living at 23, rue Jean Dolent, Paris, 14. I have written my best chapter, in the current opus, on him; it may be out now in some French revue. I sent it to his publisher, Denoel, who offered to place it for me. Madame Jean Voilier, directrice there.

Are you sure you are the first to photograph Marib? I thought either Malraux or St. Exupery had done it late in the '30's. And nearly lost their lives doing it. Ask Cendrars – he would know. Anyway, what an adventure! I do hope you will let me see one at least.

And now a word about your illness, which sounds like a very familiar one. I have two very strange, perhaps unwanted, suggestions to make. Have you ever tried a Chinese doctor? And have you heard yet about "Dianetics" (author L. Ron Hubbard)?[7] I take it yours is a "psychosomatic" ailment – about 85% of all afflictions are, even the medicos admit that to-day. This sounds naive, perhaps, but I firmly believe it is unnecessary to suffer from such an ailment. And if it's chronic, and not due to an injury, a shock (electrical) or use of drugs, you should consider approaching it from "the mind." The whole course of medicine is rapidly altering to-day, as you doubtless know. The one trend is dangerous – new drugs, brain operations, electrical shock treatment. The other, broadly "psychiatric," though I mean something much narrower, more radical, is winning over. You will pardon

me for dwelling on this, I hope. I am not a healer –
though I have healed (posing, for experiment, as an ana-
lyst, though not following the technique).[8] But in the
last ten years, all my reading, all my experiences with
people, above all, the privilege of meeting a very few
who have practised "mental healing" in one way or another, incline me to believe that so-called "medicine" is
sheer rot, futile. When I read that you are in Vichy I
conjure up the whole picture. I think it is depressing, first
of all, to be in such an environment. I can visualize these
places flourishing from one civilization to another. Perhaps minor "miracles" are achieved in these places, but
the great miracles take place elsewhere. First of all, in
one's self. You are the doctor. I know now a round dozen
eminent physicians and surgeons. What they admit about
their ignorance is appalling. Nature, they confess, takes
care of over 90% of the cases – barring injuries, I mean.
The rest – and here is a tremendous admission! – the rest
get cured *only* if they wish to! I recently read the case
against a Chinese herb doctor – probably a quack. It was
filled with testimony from "experts" – i.e. drug experts,
medicos, etc. The most negative, authoritarian statements
imaginable. I voted for the "quack." At least, he had
something to show in the way of results. The joke is that
these experts refused to consider his cures as "cures." Said
they were "remissions" – a word they fall back on when
all else fails. But when I said before – Chinese doctor –
I didn't mean an herb doctor. Inquire about "acoponc-
ture" while in Paris, if you are interested. Don't find a
"modern" Chinese doctor. And don't let any one operate
on you – unless you think you are at the point of death.
Well . . . please forgive all this!

I must stop here. Do let me know if this reaches you!
Here is to your good health – permanent good health!

> Cordially yours,
> Henry Miller

And if you do become ambassador – heartiest congratulations! Do try to meet Cendrars – write first or telephone – I think it will be rewarding. And that "Power with in us" book is about Cabeza de Vaca – a man of miracles – it should interest you much.[9]

---

[1] Written in English by Milton Mezzrow with Bernard Wolfe, the book was translated by Marcel Duhamel and Madelaine Gautier (Paris: Corrêa, 1950).

[2] 1946.

[3] Wallace Fowlie reports that the French edition and the Preface have never been published. Miller's Preface was lost; hence it could not be included in the American edition, *Love in Literature: Studies in Symbolic Expression* (Bloomington, Ind.: Indiana University Press, 1965).

[4] London: Allen & Unwin, 1943.

[5] London: Nicholson & Watson, 1946. The French edition, translated by Jean-Claude Lefaure, is *La Maison sans issues* (Paris: Courtrai, 1947).

[6] Further information on this reprinting of fragments of *Plexus* is unavailable. Volume I of *Survival* (New York), Autumn, 1950, contained "From a Book about Books."

[7] *Dianetics: The Modern Science of Mental Health* (New York: Hermitage House, 1950).

[8] Miller practiced psychoanalysis during his visit to New York from January until April, 1936.

[9] Miller apparently wrote the second page of this letter on blank space above an announcement by Abramson of the publication of a letter by Miller about the novels of Claude Houghton. Miller has written over the top of the printed matter, "And here's a typical 'Ben' announcement."

Dear Mr. Miller:

I was very happy indeed to find your letter of September 19th upon my arrival in Paris about October 1st. After writing you in Vichy my wife and I drove south into Andorra and then to Barcelona where we took a boat for Mallorca to spend a week there as my wife is urging me to find a home there when it comes time for retirement. It is a beautiful spot and life is unbelievably cheap, in comparison with the rest of the world. Furnished villas are to be had for $30 monthly and servants are in proportion but I don't fancy living on an island and I much prefer the life in France.

On our return we spent the night in Montpellier, a French town I love and there we saw another really great French movie, *Rendezvous avec la chance*.[1] I meant to send you a card from there recommending the movie in the highest terms but I never got around to it. Then I went to Paris and saw *Justice est faite*,[2] another very superior film. Seeing good French films is like reading great Russian fiction: it makes anything else pallid by comparison. Last night I was persuaded to go to see *All about Eve*,[3] on the strength of the favorable reviews. It was so artificially contrived and so lacking in the subtle touches to which I have become so accustomed in French films that I could hardly bring myself to sit through it.

While in Paris I called on Girodias and had a long talk with him. I had talked with his secretary previously and she said they had sent you the copies of translations of your books which you wanted. Abramson finally disgorged my manuscript on Tangier and I left it with Girodias who promised to read it and consider it for publication. For your strictly private information I heard in Paris that the Editions du Chene are in financial difficulties. I also ran down an illustrated copy of your Tropic of Cancer (I think it was Cancer and not Capricorn though I may be mistaken) but I did not buy it as I thought the illustrations abominable. Apparently the edition was a flop as Rombaldi had the remaindered copies which were marked down from about 5,000 to some 2,000 francs. I had a nice chat with Marcel Thiebaut, editor of the *Revue de Paris,* who has published a most favorable review of my *Restif.* My editor tells me the book has gone well in France and England but he is surprised by the absence of any demand for it from my own country.

I am reasonably satisfied I am the first to photograph Marib but one can never be sure. I should have gotten around to see Cendrars but I never got the chance. Another time. I am a bit diffident about running in on strangers.

I agree entirely with your observations on the influence of mind over matter. No, I have never tried a Chinese doctor but I did consult an Egyptian doctor about twenty years ago and was very satisfied with the results. I have heard recently of "Dianetics" and have been meaning to get the book. I will certainly do so on your recommendation. I go to Vichy less for the medical treatment than for the soothing mental influence the place has on me. It is the only place in the world I have found where I can completely relax both mentally and physically.

The voyage back to America was made on the Liberte. I arrived in New York on the 24th and have been here ever since. I had thought I would be here only a few weeks but it now looks as if I may be in this country somewhat longer. It seems definite that I shall be going to Ethiopia as ambassador. It is no promotion as I was ambassador to Saudi Arabia but the climate is infinitely better. I loved Arabia and made many friends there.

What has happened to "Plexus" and "Nexus"? I am looking forward eagerly to their appearance. When is the book on which you are now working coming out and who

will publish it? I would like to put in an advance order.
   With warm regards,

                              Yours ever,
                              J. Rives Childs

[1] French version of *Chance Meeting*, produced by J. Arthur Rank and directed by Anthony Asquith, 1954.
   [2] A French film directed by Robert Dorfman and Joseph Burstyn, 1953.
   [3] An American film directed by Joseph L. Mankiewicz, 1950.

J. R. C. to H. M., November 16, 1950   55

Dear Mr. Childs –

This will probably arrive too late – not my fault! – but hope you will come with the Howards without waiting for this!

Cordially,
Henry Miller

Dear Mr. Childs –

Did you ever get the items I sent you via the Howards[1]
– with telegram & letter delivered too late, alas?

Just read "Sara" (John Rodker edition).[2] First taste of
Restif – and a powerful one. Can see what you mean
now. Still hoping to get "Monsieur Nicolas" et "Les Nuits
de Paris."

Henry   Miller

[1] What these items were is not known.
[2] *Sara,* tr. R. Crowdy Mathers (London: John Rodker, 1927).

Dear Mr. Miller:

I must ask you to forgive me for my silence. Since returning from my trip I have been sitting on a Board here
on which I have had to work frequently at night and I
have just recently had the first respite from my labors.

Yes, I did receive the items you sent me and I am most
grateful for them. You may be neglected by your own
generation but you will surely come into your own, as
surely as Restif has after his years of neglect.

I am happy you have finally cut your teeth on Restif.
"Sara" is a cry from the heart and one of the most powerful things he ever did. The version you have read is that
taken from his autobiography, *Monsieur Nicolas.* He
wrote it first in a somewhat more extended form under
the title, *La Derniere Aventure d'un Homme de Qua-
rante-cinq Ans.*[1] Personally, I prefer the first and fuller
version.

Sara was a perfect little bitch who led Restif around
by the nose, as so many of her kind have done to other
men before and since.

I must try to find *Monsieur Nicolas* and the *Nuits* for
you when I am in France. I sail on the 23rd on the Liberté, will be a few days in Paris, and then go to Rome for
a few weeks before proceeding to my new post. It is not
official yet but I hope to receive my orders in the next
six weeks. You should hear from me next from the land of
Rimbaud.

I was sorry not to have seen you in California. Your
card came only after we had left. I had some hesitancy

in intruding upon you without knowing whether it would be convenient.

With warm regards and every good wish,

Sincerely yours,
J. Rives Childs

---

[1] Geneva, 1783. See Childs, *Restif*, pp. 282–83.

Dear Mr. Childs –

I was indeed delighted to receive "Les Nuits de Paris" the other day. Have begun reading it. I see that I shall end by reading every thing of Restif's I can lay hands on. How right you were to keep after me in this connection! "Sara," incidentally, still reverberates in me. I began, you know, with Strindberg's "Le Plaidoyer d'un Fou"[1] – at the age of 18. That was tapping "the main line," so to speak. Reread it the other day. How intimate and familiar! And a wonderful bare style, as has Restif in "Sara," I notice. (And Gorky, to mention an "outsider.")

I am waiting to hear from you again – from Abysinnia [*sic*], to hear you have come upon some souvenirs of Rimbaud.

Plexus, which you asked about, I just signed a contract for with Corréa, Paris – for the French version. Don't know yet who will bring it out in English. (I knew of my publisher's difficulties – alas, only too well.)

The book about books, which I've finally decided to call "The Plains of Abraham," will come out this Fall, by New Directions, and simultaneously in England, I understand. I think you will like this first volume. A fragment from it (on "Influences") appeared, in French, in a Tunisian revue – *U49–51.* If you'd like a copy, write to Monsieur Albert Maillet – 5, Place de la République, Vienne (*Isère*) France. The "World Review" London published the chapter on Blaise Cendrars in the Feb. and March issues (1951). Denoël is bringing out this same chapter in a handsome *plaquette* (illustrated) with a few words of "hommage" by Cendrars, I am told.[2]

I am now compiling my list of "books read" for insertion in the first or last volume of the book on books. Quite a job! Yet less than 5,000 titles. But all dug up from memory. A fool's task, I suppose – yet I have never seen it done by another writer. I think it will give pleasure to *some* readers.

After that – *on verra.* Perhaps I will begin writing *Nexus,* a long, long, volume – the hardest to do. It terrifies me, frankly.

Well, I wait eagerly to hear from you again.

I trust you are now in good health.

Henry Miller

---

[1] Strindberg wrote the prose work, *Le Plaidoyer d'un fou,* in French in 1887–88; it was first published in 1895.

[2] The title of the book when it appeared in 1952 was *The Books in My Life* (see Letter 29). The list of "books read" mentioned in the next paragraph of the letter did not appear in the English, though it made the French, edition (see Letter 52). The fragments from the book mentioned by Miller are as follows: "Lectures and Influences," *U-49-51: Revue littéraire mensuelle,* Nos. 5 and 6 (Jan., Feb., 1951); "Blaise Cendrars," *World Review,* n.s. 24 (Feb., 1951); "More about Blaise Cendrars," *ibid.* (March, 1951); *Blaise Cendrars,* tr. François Villié ([Paris]: Denoël, [1951]).

Dear Mr. Miller:

Here I am in the land of Rimbaud. I arrived on the fifth, coming down the Red Sea by boat and up from Djibouti by train – and what a strange and fascinating land it is! I am entranced. Coming up from Djibouti we glimpsed all manner of animals such as baboons, gazelle and birds of a most beautiful plumage. The landscape is African and unlike anything I had ever seen before.

Addis lies on the slopes of the mountains and is spread out over a large area with immense eucalyptus trees soaring to great heights and obscuring the mud-brick homes of the natives and the more imposing official buildings and residences of the foreign colony. It is delightfully cool – a bit too cool for me after Jidda – and we are on the verge of the rainy season when it rains daily for several months. But I have my books with me and as long as I have those I am happy anywhere.

I have begun to read Enid Starkie's "Rimbaud in Abysinnia"[1] and am anxious to learn more of Rimbaud.[2] What particular books concerning him would you especially recommend?

I am so happy to hear that "Plexus" is on its way and I shall be most interested in knowing when it may be published. I do hope that it may be shortly available in English but if not I shall arrange to obtain the French translation. You must get to work on "Nexus." I shall certainly obtain "The Plains of Abraham" when it appears.

Am so glad you liked the "Nuits de Paris." I knew you would. You will like "Monsieur Nicolas" even more because you will find yourself all through it. I wish I could have found the Liseux or the Jonquieres edition but I couldn't. Some time when you have read more of Restif you must do an appreciation of him. But don't do it until you have read "Monsieur Nicolas," one of the very great books of the world.

I am reading now the quatrains of Abu el Ala, the greatest of the Arabian poets and one who must have inspired Omar Khayyam.[3] This is the epitaph he asked to be inscribed on his tomb:

> This wrong was by my father done
> To me, but ne'er by me to one.

This must do for the moment but I shall be writing you again and telling you more of Ethiopia which reminds me in so many ways of Persia and Morocco.

All good wishes to you.

Yours ever,
J. Rives Childs

[1] *Rimbaud in Abyssinia* (Oxford: Clarendon Press, 1937).

[2] Childs was later to find that the memory Rimbaud had left in Ethiopia was as fugitive as that left by T. E. Lawrence in Arabia.

[3] Abu-l-Ala al-Maari (973–1057), freethinking poet and philosopher, was born near Aleppo. Some of his poetry was first translated into English by Ameen F. Rihani and published in London by Grant Richards (*The Quatrains of Abu'l-Ala,* 1904).

Dear Mr. Childs –

By all means read Rimbaud's "Lettres d'Abyssinie" edited by Enid Starkie.[1] Also Jacques Rivière's "Rimbaud" and "Rimbaud le Voyant" by A. Rolland de Renéville – or even "La Vie de Rimbaud" (popular but good) by Jean-Marie Carré.[2] My books on books will be called (new title) "My Life with Books" – publisher's suggestion. (New Directions – this Fall.) Yes, I intend definitely to read *all* of "Monsieur Nicolas." The fragments I read of "Nuits de Paris" were not as good as *Sara*, I thought. But he is my man, yes!

What a fascinating world you are in – Ethiopia! I wish I were there. *Harrar* is a place identified with Rimbaud.

You ought to have a look at a most interesting book called "L'Etrange XXᵉ Siècle" by Dr. de Fontbrune (Michelet, Editeur: Sarlat (Dordogne) France).[3]

I hope you won't forget to send me a picture post card occasionally. I treasure them.

And I hope you are now in good health!

Good wishes,
Henry Miller

[1] Enid Starkie has not edited a book by this title. Perhaps Miller is referring to the French edition of *Rimbaud in Abyssinia* (Paris: Payot, 1938), which quoted, Starkie says, "a great many unpublished letters." Or the reference may be to *Lettres de Jean-Arthur Rimbaud* (*Egypte, Arabie, Ethiopie*) published by Rimbaud's brother-in-law in 1899.

[2] All three books were published in Paris, Rivière's by Kra in 1930 Renéville's by Au Sans Pareil in 1929 (enl. ed. by Le Colombe in 1947), and Carré's by Plon in 1926 (enl. ed., 1949).

[3] 1950.

Dear Mr. Miller:

I recently received the Autumn number of the Arizona
quarterly containing a most interesting article by Harold
Maine on you and I feel sure that I owe it to your
kind thought that a copy of this interesting article was
sent me which I enjoyed very thoroughly.[1] If you have
occasion to write to Mr. Maine, I wish you would extend
my hearty congratulations to him and tell him how much
I appreciated his piece.

Sometime ago you expressed the desire for postcards
of Ethiopia. I tried to obtain some at the time but the
single shop which sells them was out of stock. I do not
get down to town very often but the other day I did so
and I obtained a number which I am enclosing and which
I hope you will like and which may please at the
same time your little girl.

Is there any news about "Book About Books" about
which you have written me in the past, if not let me
know when it is published and if so I would like to
send for a copy.

Life goes on much the same way here. I have man-
aged to get out and see a little of the country and in the
next few weeks I expect to do more travelling.

I have been working on a new book myself since I last
wrote you. It is called "Operation Torch: An Object Les-
son in Diplomacy," and it is the diplomatic background
of the events leading up to the North African Landings.[2]
I had to submit it to the Department for approval and
the first reaction was extremely favorable which I received at the end of December. Unfortunately it has to
pass through many hands in Washington and I have
heard nothing about its fate since. I think it is a good book
and that it should have a wide reading public both in

the United States and France. If and when it appears I shall see that you receive a copy.

Is there any further news on additional volumes of the "Rosy Crucificion"??

With every good wish and kind regards,

Sincerely yours,
J. Rives Childs

P.S. You may continue to write me at APO 843 c/o Postmaster, New York City

---

[1] Harold Maine, "Henry Miller: Bigotry's Whipping Boy," *Arizona Quarterly*, VII (Autumn, 1951), 197–208.

[2] "Operation Torch" remains unpublished (1968) although it was cleared by the State Department for publication after the war. Childs was privy to the plans for the Allied invasion of North Africa and gives a detailed account of them and of the diplomatic aftermath.

Dear Mr. Miller:

   You will probably be wondering why I have not acknowledged sooner your thoughtfulness in having your
publishers send me a copy of *Plexus*.[1] The fact is I have
just returned from two months in France and Spain
and did not find the book until I reached Addis.

   I was wandering about Nice soon after my arrival
when I saw a copy of *Plexus* displayed in a bookstore
(you will be interested to know it is very widely displayed). I made inquiry whether an English edition was
available or was likely to be shortly and could obtain no
answer. I then wrote to my book dealer in Paris and
asked him to make inquiry and to send me a copy of the
French edition if no English edition was expected soon.
He has not replied as yet.

   Just now I am in the midst of reading it and I like all
that I have read. I am not yet able to judge whether I like
it as well as your *Tropic of Cancer* or *Max and the White
Phagocytes* (one of the best things you have ever written
was in the latter; I mean "Via Dieppe – New Haven").[2]

   Will you satisfy my curiosity and let me know when an
English edition of *Plexus* may be expected?

   I judge there have been cuts in the French edition,
as there were in the French edition of *Sexus*. Will the
English edition preserve the original text, and were the
cuts many?[3]

   While in Paris I interested Gallimard in my "Operation: Torch" and they are going to read it.[4] I have also
interested a French publisher in bringing out a new and
more complete edition of Casanova than has ever hitherto
been issued. I have been busy in research on Casanova
and have made some discoveries which I believe will
set the savants by the ears. If anything is published I
will see that you receive a copy but the new edition of

Casanova I have in mind will take a year or more to complete. To my mind his *Memoirs* are one of the great books of the world. I have been able to add a full volume to the twelve hitherto known.[5]

It has been a long time since I had news of you. I do hope you and your family are well. And that all goes happily with you.

Have you ever read Amiel's *Journal?*[6] I picked it up again last night after thirty years and found it as stimulating as when I read it in my youth. I wish we could get together some time and talk nothing but books. What has become of your book on books?

All the very best to you.

J. Rives Childs

[1] Tr. Elisabeth Guertic (Paris: Corrêa, 1952).

[2] *Max and the White Phagocytes* (Paris: Obelisk Press, [1938]), pp. 205–37.

[3] Miller answers in the next letter.

[4] Gallimard's readers approved the book, but it was finally rejected on the ground of limited appeal.

[5] Childs has not published a new edition of Casanova's memoirs as yet (1968), but some of his new material appears in his *Casanova: A Biography Based on New Documents* (London: Allen & Unwin, 1961) and even more in the French translation by Francis-L. Mars of his *Casanova, Biographie nouvelle, d'après des documents inédits* (Paris: Pauvert, 1962). Current discoveries are made known in his *Casanova Gleanings,* issued under his editorship annually.

[6] 1882. Childs recalls that he read Mrs. Humphry Ward's translation of the *Journal intime* (London and New York: Macmillan, 1885).

Dear Mr. Childs –

First chance I've had to answer your recent letter. "Plexus" is not yet contracted for in English, but probably will be taken by my old French publisher, now La Nouvelle Soc. des Ed. du Chêne (a Hachette subsidiary.) There was one cut of 2 or 3 pages only, as I recall, and it was not important. There *was* an unexpurgated edition of Sexus but only a few hundred got out into hands of critics. (*In French*).

"The Books in My Life" is now out, in England and U.S.A. If you'd like a copy, order of *me* – it will help. Price is $5.00.

Cancer & Capricorn are now to appear in Danish as well as German, and Black Spring in Swedish. *Plexus* in Italian.[1] Yes, I read *Amiel* years ago – and speak of it in my new book.

All's well here after many tribulations – and separation from my wife.

My best always,
Henry Miller

P.S. The Rimbaud book is out too – in French, – Editions Mermod, Lausanne (Suisse) – nice edition.

---

[1] The two translations of *Cancer* were *Krebsens Vendekrebs,* tr. Jørgen Rothenborg (Copenhagen: Casper Nielsens, 1953), and *Wendekreis des Krebses,* tr. Kurt Wagenseil (Hamburg: Rowohlt, 1952), and of *Capricorn, Stenbukkens Vendekreds,* tr. Jørgen Rothenborg (Copenhagen: Hans Reitzel, 1955), and *Wendekreis des Steinbocks* (Hamburg: Rowohlt, 1953). The translator of the latter is not known but it may have been Kurt Wagenseil. *Black Spring* was first published by the Obelisk Press in Paris in 1936. The Swedish translation by Lars Gustav Hellström was *Svart Vår* (Stockholm: Hugo Gebers, 1952). Henry Furst did the Italian translation of *Plexus* (Milan: Longanesi, 1955).

Dear Mr. Miller:

I have just received your letter of September 15 and was delighted to have news of you and of your work. Your letter arrived at a most opportune time as I was just about to order, "The Books in My Life." I enclose a check for $5.00. Please send it to me addressed: J. Rives Childs, American Embassy, A.P.O. 843, c/o Postmaster, New York City.

I shall send you shortly an article of mine on Casanova which is being published by the Bibliographical Society of America.[1] I have just finished reading the proofs. I am working on a number of other projects and will let you know when they have matured. I am off tomorrow for Asmara for about three weeks in connection with the Federation ceremonies or I would have written you somewhat more at length.[2]

With warm regards and every good wish,

Sincerely yours,
J. Rives Childs

---

[1] "Clue to the Mystery of Casanova's Memoirs (A)," in Bibliographical Society of America, *Papers*, XLVI (1952), 287–326.
[2] The federation of Ethiopia and Eritrea.

Dear Mr. Miller:

I want to tell you how much I have enjoyed BOOKS ABOUT BOOKS. I have not finished it because it is too fine to swallow in a gulp. I was tempted to but I limit myself to a few pages a night in order to savor it the more thoroughly.

My greatest disappointment in the book is to learn that you don't care for Shakespeare and Poe and you apparently are unfamiliar with Chekhov. Gautier in one of the most memorable of his sketches about his artistic friends in Paris tells of one young man of his acquaintance who never wrote or painted but who won a position for himself and was universally acclaimed for his accomplishments which were thus heralded on his tombstone: HE LOVED SHAKESPEARE.[1]

I was fortunate to be introduced to Shakespeare by my mother and two great scholars of English literature: Dr. Blackwell of Randolph-Macon College,[2] and George Lyman Kittredge of Harvard. I spent two years studying six plays of Shakespeare each year. For me he is the immortal of immortals. If I were obliged to choose four authors to whom I would have to confine my reading for the rest of my life I would choose them in this order: Shakespeare, Casanova's Memoirs, and Chekhov.[3]

In your BOOK ABOUT BOOKS you express an interest in learning something of erotic literature. As I have tried during my life to pursue almost every branch of reading I have gained some knowledge of that field.

I cite for you first of all the bibliographies, as follows:

1) *Bibliographie des ouvrages relatif a l'amour* etc., fourth edition, in four large volumes;[4]

2) Pisanus Fraxi, Index Librorum Prohibitorum etc., three vol.[5]

3) Reade, Registrum Librorum Eroticorum[6]

4) Perceau, Bibliographie du roman erotique au XIX Siecle, 2 vol., covering the French field only.[7]

5) Carrington, Forbidden Books[8]

Incidentally I have all these.

The greatest erotic writer I know is André de Nerciat and I put his *Felicia* at the top of the list. His best other works are: *Les Aphrodites, le Diable au Corps, le Doctorat Impromptu*, and *le Noviciat de Lolotte*.[9] Emile Henriot has a charming essay on de Nerciat in his *Livres du Second Rayon*.[10]

Among other first class works I would put: *My Secret Life*,[11] Restif's *Anti-Justine*, de Sade's *Juliette* and *Justine*,[12] and the following anonymous works: *Education d'une demi-vierge, Eveline, Fleurs Lascives*,[13] *Hic et Hec, le Libertin de Qualite* of Mirabeau,[14] Apollinaire's *Exploits d'un jeune Don Juan*,[15] Pigault-Lebrun's *l'Enfant d'un Bordel*,[16] Diderot's *les Bijoux Indiscrets*,[17] *le Portier des Chartreux*,[18] *le Rideau Levé*,[19] *Tableaux Vivants*,[20] *Thérèse Philosophe, Venus in India, Parisian Frolics, Mémoires d'une Chanteuse Allemande* (probably the most revealing memoirs ever written by a woman), Chorier's *Dialogues de Luisa Sigea*,[21] and an unpublished manuscript I have seen entitled *Unmotherly Love* which in my opinion is on a par with any of the foregoing.[22]

In a second category I would place the following: *Confessions of Nemesis Hunt*,[23] *L'Ecole des Biches, Un Eté à la Campagne*,[24] *Flossie* (believed to have been written by Swinburne),[25] *Forbidden Fruit*,[26] *Gamiani*, said to have been written by de Musset and George Sand in collaboration,[27] Pierre Louys' *Histoire du Roi Gonzalve*,[28] Montbron's *Margot la Ravaudeuse*,[29] *Memoirs of Dolly Morton*,[30] *Mes Amours avec Victoire*,[31] *A Night in a Moorish Harem*,[32] and a good many more in the two series *Bibliothèque de l'Amour* et *Coffret du Bibliophile*.[33] I should not omit the Arabian Nights in either the Burton or Mardrus translations and, of course, that Chinese classic *Ching Ping M'ei*.[34]

In the foregoing list I have really only scratched the surface.

The French as you know make a charming distinction between works which are *galant* and those which are *libre*. De Nerciat's *Felicia* is *galant* rather than *libre*, while others are on the borderline or may be a mixture of both. My list omits for the most part purely pornographic works although there are a few mentioned such as *Forbidden Fruit, Mes Amours avec Victoire, le Portier des Chartreux,* the *Rideau Levé, Parisian Frolics,* and *Unmotherly Love*. Let me put it this way and that is I would say there is something in these pornographic works which gives them some [literary] distinction among their vile counterparts; indeed *le Rideau Levé* has been attributed to Mirabeau.

I would like some day to write a study of the *galant* and *libre* in literature and perhaps I may do so.[35]

In the meantime if you have any questions on the subject which you think I might answer I will do my best.

Your publishers sent me a bill for $5.28 for the BOOK ABOUT BOOKS and as I only remitted you $5 I am enclosing thirty cents in stamps.

I am leaving here on January 18th and am going to settle in Nice. My address after the first of the year will be in care of the American Consulate there.

All the best to you.

J. Rives Childs

[1] See Letter 21, note 2.

[2] Robert Emory Blackwell served as professor of English at Randolph-Macon College, Ashland, Va., from 1876 until 1938. For the last thirty-six of those years he was also president of the College.

[3] As originally typed, Childs listed Shakespeare, Chekhov, Casanova's memoirs, and Henry Miller. Then he apparently wanted to

change the order and crossed out Chekhov and Miller. He rewrote Chekhov above Miller's name, leaving only three authors.

[4] [Jules Gay,] *Bibliographie des principaux ouvrages relatifs à l'amour, aux femmes, au mariage,* . . . 4th ed., rev. and enl., by J. Lemonnyer (Paris [Vol. I], Lille [Vols. II–IV], 1894–1900).

[5] Henry Spencer Ashbee (pseud., Pisanus Fraxi) compiled three books, all privately printed in London: *Index librorum prohibitorum, being notes bio-biblio-icono-graphical and critical, on curious and uncommon books* (1877), *Centuria librorum absconditorum* . . . (1879), and *Catena librorum tacendorum* . . . (1885).

[6] Alfred Rose (pseud., Rolf S. Reade), *Registrum librorum eroticorum, vel (sub hac specie) dubiorum* . . . (2 v., London: Privately printed, 1936).

[7] Louis Perceau, *Bibliographie du roman érotique au XIXe siècle* . . . (2 v.; Paris, 1930).

[8] Charles Carrington's work was privately printed (Paris, 1902).

[9] Early editions of the books by Robert André de Nerciat mentioned by Childs are: *Félicia; ou, Mes fredaines* (2 v.; London, 1775); *Les Aphrodites* (Brussels, 1793); *Le Diable au corps* (3 v.; Paris, 1803); *Le Doctorat impromptu* (Brussels, 1788), and *Mon noviciat; ou, Les Joies de Lolotte* (2 v.; Berlin, 1792). The bibliographical information about these and the following works (notes 10–32) is offered as the best obtainable from available resources at the present time.

[10] Paris, 1926.

[11] 11 v.; Amsterdam, [1894]; author unknown. Childs obtained the set now at the Institute for Sex Research, Inc., Indiana University, which was used by the Grove Press for their recent edition.

[12] Marquis de Sade, *Juliette; ou, Les Prosperités du vice* (6 v.; Hollande [Paris], 1797) and *Justine; ou, Les Malheurs de la vertu* (4 v.; Hollande [Paris], 1791).

[13] *Éducation* (2 v.; Brussels, 1903); *Eveline* (or *Evelina*); *or, The Amours and Adventures of a Lady of Fashion* (2 v.; London, c.1840); *Fleurs lascives* (*La Fleur lascive orientale* [Oxford, 1882]).

[14] *Hic et Hec; ou, L'Éleve des RR. PP. Jésuites d'Avignon* (Berlin, 1798) has been attributed to Honoré Gabriel Riqueti, Comte de Mirabeau, whose *Libertin* appeared in London in 1783.

[15] *Les Mémoires d'un jeune Don Juan* (Paris, 1907). Subsequent editions bore the title *Les Exploits d'un jeune Don Juan*.

[16] The attribution of *L'Enfant du bordel* (Paris, 1800) to Pigault-Lebrun (pseud. of Charles Antoine Guillaume Pigault de l'Éniney) is not certain.

[17] Denis Diderot, *Les Bijoux indiscrets* (2 v.; Pekin, 1748).

[18] Jean Charles Gervaise de Latouche, *Histoire de Dom B . . . Portier des Chartreux* (Rome, c.1745).

[19] *Le Rideau levé; ou, L'Éducation de Laure* (2 v.; Cythère [Alençon], 1786), often attributed to Mirabeau, is by the Marquis de Sentilly.

[20] Paul Perret, *Les Tableaux vivants; ou, Mes confessions aux pieds de la duchesse . . .* (Amsterdam, 1870).

[21] *Thérèse* (The Hague, 1748); Capt. Charles Devereaux, pseud., *Venus in India* (Paris, 1895); *Parisian Frolics* (London, 1896); *Aus den Memoiren einer Saengerin* (2 pts.; [Altona, Hamburg,] c.1868, 1875); and Nicolas Chorier (pseud., Luisa Sigea), *Aloisiae Sigaeae Toletana Satyra sotadica de arcanis amoris & veneris* (Amsterdam, 1660).

[22] Author unknown.

[23] London, 1907.

[24] Only one author is known of *École* (Paris, 1863) and of *Été* (Brussels, 1867). Edmond Duponchel and two collaborators hid their authorship of *École* under the pseudonyms Chapuys, Bokel, and d'Enghien. Poulet-Malassis was one of two authors of *Été*.

[25] *Flossie* was published in London (the title page gives "Carnapolis") in 1897.

[26] The author of *Forbidden Fruit, Luscious and Exciting Story,* and *More Forbidden Fruit; or, Master Percy's Progress in and beyond the Domestic Circle* (London, 1905) is not known.

[27] Alfred de Musset and George Sand used the pseudonym Alcide Baron de M . . . for *Gamiani* (Brussels, 1833).

[28] Louys's work was *Histoire du roi Gonzalve et des douze princesses* (Paris, 1927).

[29] Fougerat de Montbron's *Margot* appeared in Hamburg in 1772.

[30] Paris, 1899, perhaps by Hugues Rebell.

[31] Probably by Edmond Dumoulin (Amsterdam, 1888).

[32] London, c.1890; ostensibly by Lord George Herbert.

[33] The "Maîtres de l'amour" was a series of reprints of "galant" or erotic classics under the direction of G. Apollinaire and B. Villeneuve. They were published by the Bibliothèque des Curieux, Paris, 1910–34. "Le Coffret du bibliophile" was a similar series issued by the same publisher from 1905 to 1959.

[34] The Burton translation was issued in 10 volumes and 6 supplementary volumes by the Kamashastra Society for private subscribers only (Benares, 1885). The Casanova Society published Dr. J. C. Mardrus' translation (collated by E. Powys Mathers) in 8 volumes (London, 1923). *Ching Ping M'ei* dates from about 1560.

[35] A member of the Institute for Sex Research founded by Dr. A. C. Kinsey wrote Mr. Childs on June 8, 1954: "To my limited

J. R. C. to H. M., November 17, 1952

knowledge there are only a handful of people who have any scholarly knowledge of erotic books and every one of these is in or beyond his fifth decade of life. I fear that the next fifteen or twenty years will see this knowledge lost."

Dear Mr. Childs –

Wondering if you are at Nice now. If so, perhaps we can meet, either here or in Nice, before Friday. Doubt if we shall stay longer than Friday. Have been in France since New Year's Day. May now go to Italy for a few weeks, until the weather changes. Am waiting for word from my Italian publisher (Mondadori in Milano) as to a place to go to – somewhere where it is warm, a few comforts, and not too expensive. Everything in France costs outrageously, I find. My money just melts.

Incidentally, do you know how many francs you are allowed to take with you in crossing the border? Also, should you have any suggestions to make, as to a good place to stay in Italy, please tell me. I don't know a word of Italian, unfortunately. Perhaps my French will carry me through. I keep wondering how Amalfi would be – do you know?

Well, this will probably be a bit of a surprise for you. I trust all goes well with you – and that we may meet.

Sincerely yours,
Henry Miller

Dear Mr. Childs –

Your wife was kind enough to telephone me and told me you are expected in Nice Sunday. We expect to leave here Sunday for la Ciotat. Will let you know exact address when we get there – or, if I know it to-morrow, I will leave it with the porter here at the hotel. Have given up the idea of going to Italy – find it's just as expensive there as here. Can't get used to these fantastic prices. Will probably return to Big Sur, via Paris, in a month or two.

All good wishes!

Henry Miller

P.S. Is the franc going to be devaluated, do you think? Fantastic that one can buy a $20.00 gold piece for fifty dollars (in francs) – just for security's sake! The whole world economy is absolutely crazy.

Dear Mr. Miller:

I was very much distressed upon my arrival on February 3, 1953 to find that you had been so near and that I had missed you. I telephoned the hotel and learned that you had gone. I am sending this to the Hotel Bristol in the hope that it will be forwarded.

My wife and I have just found an apartment, which suits us, in Nice and I only wish it were so that we were in it to be able to entertain you but I hope this will be for another time. You did not give me your address in La Ciotat and unfortunately my car is in Paris so that I cannot come to see you. I am leaving for Paris about the 22nd to get my car and if you are going to be in Southern France for any time I shall run over and pay you a visit. Do let me know your plans. I am for the moment at the Hotel Adriatic where I shall be for at least two weeks. After that I suggest that you write me in care of the American Consulate in Nice.

With warm regards and hoping very much that I shall have the pleasure of meeting you at long last, believe me.

> Very sincerely yours,
> J. Rives Childs

La Ciotat (Bouches-du-Rhône),
France; February 13, 1953 ♈

Dear Mr. Childs –

I hope to be here until the 21st and then leave for
Vienne (Isere) where I have a good friend. I am just a
little uncertain, however, as it seems I am wanted in Paris
by the Juge d'Instruction – because of the "Sexus" publication. A stay of time has been requested – till the end
of March – and perhaps it will be granted.

If you return by car from Paris you might see if we are
at 5, Place de la République, Vienne – chez Albert Maillet.

My agent in Paris, Dr. Michael A. Hoffman – 77 Blvd.
St. Michel – would always know my whereabouts.

About the "Sexus" business, please consider this confidential.

Somewhere then, some time soon, I do expect to meet
you.

> With sincere regards –
> Henry Miller

Dear Mr. Childs –

We are going by car, with our friends here, next Saturday and Sunday, to Geneva and Lausanne. Will be back Sunday night. Thought I ought to tell you as you may just be passing through here when we are away.

If we don't see you here we probably will in Paris – some time later. Hope to stay in France till June or July at least.

The only thing I worry about is the imminent Russian invasion of Europe. By all signs it is due soon. I shouldn't like to be caught in it! If ever you get any authentic warning, do let me know immediately. My mail address will always be –

c/o Dr. Michael A. Hoffman
77 Blvd. Saint-Michel
Paris (5°)

> With all good wishes –
> Cordially,
> Henry Miller

P.S. I go before the Juge d'Instruction towards end of March. Hope to get off with a light (!) fine, at the worst.
P.P.S. "Plexus" is now coming out in English, in Paris – 3 months hence and "Hamlet" in *French* – by Corrêa[1] –towards end of year, I guess.

---

[1] *Hamlet* [abridged], tr. Roger Giroux (Paris: Corrêa, 1956).

My dear Mr. Childs –

I've been back here since the early part of August. Was on the go constantly while over there. Most wonderful experience for me – this return. May go abroad again next September, for a year, via Japan, India, Palestine. Hope then to see you, wherever you will be.

The Olympia Press, Paris (M. Girodias) brought out "Plexus" in 2-vols. – *unexpurgated*. Think edition is now exhausted. The Germans have brought out the Tropics and will issue 3 or 4 others shortly. Now the Swedes want the Tropics – and the Danes! The Japanese have taken about seven books, including all the banned ones – some to be put out in English as well (for our G I's).[1] And in Feb. or March Corrëa, Paris, will bring out "Hamlet" (with Michael Fraenkel) – reduced by ⅓ – to make *one* vol.

I am now on *Nexus* – but working slowly. Too many interruptions here. The trial (of "Sexus") comes up in Paris soon. Maître Sev of Passy is defending me. Here, in S.F. (U.S.) the courts decided for a second time the Tropics *are* obscene *etc*. And they insulted me royally! But all this only stimulates sales and translations. What fools they are! I now have the complete set of "Monsieur Nicolas" – a gift from an admirer. Haven't the heart to tackle it yet.

All good wishes to you and to Madame Childs.

Henry Miller

---

[1] *Cancer* and *Capricorn* appeared in Swedish translation – *Kräftans Vändkrets* and *Stenbocken Vändkrets*, tr. Sven Lundgren (Stockholm: Central Press, 1956). By 1955 the following titles had been published in Japan (Tokyo) in English by Keimeisha: *Black Spring* (1954), *Plexus*, Vol. II only (1954), *Sexus* (2 v.; 1953), *Tropic of*

Cancer (1953), and *Tropic of Capricorn* (1953). By the same date the Japanese translations, all published in Tokyo by Shincho-sha, were *The Air-conditioned Nightmare,* tr. Yasuo Ōkubo (1954), *Black Spring,* tr. Ken'ichi Yoshida (1954), *Rimbaud,* tr. Shigeya Konishi (1955), *Sexus* (1955–   ), *The Smile at the Foot of the Ladder* (1954), *The Tropic of Cancer* (1954), *The Tropic of Capricorn* (1955), and *The World of Sex,* tr. Ken'ichi Yoshida (1953). The names of the translators of several of these volumes are not available.

Dear Henry Miller:

   Your letter of December 19th turned up today (there
have been more postal strikes) and I was delighted to
have news of you. I was so distressed that we couldn't get
together last year. If and when you come back arrange to
come to Nice where we shall be happy to put you up for
a week or ten days or as long as you care to stay. We
have a car and can take you wherever you want to go.
You must let me know in advance so I shall be sure to
be here and not traveling somewhere as we frequently do.
   I am glad also to have news of your literary progress.
I have the two volumes of PLEXUS in English, and I
also have the complete HAMLET, in fact, I don't think
there is any book of yours I do not have. It's a pity we
can't grow up at home; we are still so terribly immature.
That is one of the reasons I came to France to live. I felt
I couldn't live anywhere else with any real pleasure. I
was at home from September 30th to November 17th: a
month at my old home in Virginia.
   You are going to like MONSIEUR NICOLAS, but
take it slowly and savor it, a few pages a day. Books
shouldn't be taken at a gulp any more than food. I am
now reading Richelieu's MEMOIRS in six volumes.[1] I
can't understand how I ever neglected them for so long.
They sparkle by the wit and charm of the narrative: all
diamonds and no rubbish. Books and friends are my
greatest joys in life. A friend will sometimes fail you but
not a good book; a friend will sometimes bore you but
not the great masters such as Shakespeare, Chekhov, and
Casanova (I know you don't like Shakespeare but I had
the good fortune to study him under one of the greatest
Shakespearean scholars, George Lyman Kittredge and it
is the part of my formal education I look back upon
with the greatest pleasure).

I hope NEXUS will not be too long in the womb. SEXUS and PLEXUS are very great poems; they have an epic sweep.

If I can help you over here call on me; don't look upon me as a friend in name only. If you want any hard-to-get books send me a list; I am in bookstores every day, or if you want any help in any other way let me know.

All the very best and here's hoping we meet in 1954.

JRC

---

[1] Baron de Lamothe-Langon, *Mémoires historiques et anecdotiques du duc de Richelieu* (Paris: Marne, 1829).

Dear friend,

Your letter of January 7th, which I meant to answer
in a few days, I have only gotten to now. Incredible
how little time I have living in this supposedly secluded
spot! In August it will be a year that we are back. It is
just possible we may get over again this Fall, for a full
year's stay abroad. But this time I may go via Japan, India, Greece, Palestine to France. It depends on how well
my books go in Japan, where they are being published,
some in English as well as Japanese. (The banned ones
in two versions.) I wonder, by the way, if you will still
be in Nice? And – do you ever run into Michel Simon, the
movie actor? I thought him a most wonderful individual.

In Paris I have a good friend in the libraire, Pierre
Laleure, who has a small shop in the 17th arrondisse-
ment. Recently I asked him for several books – he usually
digs up anything I ask for – but haven't had a response
from him in six weeks or more. I begin to fear that something has happened to him. Anyway, there are two authors
I am interested in at the moment and their books are
hard to get. One is "Pourquoi je suis bouddhiste" par
Maurice Magre.[1] The other is the two sequels to "Les
Trois Totemisations" par Lotus de Paini.[2] The one
named, which I've just read, was published by Chacornac,
Paris, but I am not sure that the other two were also,
nor can I, alas, give you the titles of these two. I was most
impressed by the first. More than that, I will say. There
is a little revue appearing irregularly, called "Le Goeland"
published in Brittany at Paramé, I think – it was through
that I ran across her name. (A pen name – right name
is Peralte.) If in your rambles thru the Nicois bookshops
you should stumble on any of these I would be delighted
if you'd mail them to me and let me know what I owe

you. (Provided it's not a too exorbitant price they want for Paini's works!)

Of all the books I was searching for, when writing "The Books in My Life," the only one I could not lay hands on was "The Thirteen Crucified Saviours" by Sir Godfrey Higgins. It exists, in England, but at prohibitive figures. You may know of him as author of a celebrated work called "Anacalypsis," dealing with Isis.[3] I don't know if he's worth the effort to get hold of, but I certainly am intrigued.

I notice that the trial of "Sexus" has not come off yet. My hunch is that it never will. I appeared before the judge in Paris and was most considerately treated. The book is still outlawed. But it may be republished, in English, in Denmark or Holland; meanwhile it's out – pirated twice – in Japan. Thus the censors continue to defeat themselves.

Well, I trust this finds you in good spirits. I know you are deep in some lengthy work. I wish I had your appetite and capacity for such herculean labors.

Cordially yours,
Henry Miller

And my respects to Madame Childs whose voice I remember over the telephone.

---

[1] Paris: Éditions de France, 1928.

[2] Lotus de Paini (pseud. of Lotus Péralté), *Les Trois Totemisations* (Paris: Chacornac Frères, 1924); the sequels are *La Magie et le mystère de la femme* (Paris: Éditions du Loup, 1928) and *Pierre Volonté* (Paris: Éditions Leymarie, 1932).

[3] The place and date of publication of Higgins' *The Thirteen Crucified Saviours* have not been found. His *Anacalypsis, an Attempt to Draw Aside the Veil of the Saitic Isis; or, An Inquiry into the Origin of Languages, Nations, and Religions* was published in 2 volumes in London in 1836. It has been reprinted a number of times, for example, by Macy-Masius in New York in 1927.

My dear friend:

I have had your letter of April 23, 1954, on my desk these
many months. Why have I not replied? – the answer is
simple; I have been trying in vain to find the book by
Magre you wanted and the two books of Lotus de Paini.
I have been hoping from one month to another that I
would have something definite to report but, alas, my efforts until now have proved fruitless.

A few days ago a young librarian came in to see me
and I told him what I was looking for and he promised
his help. I make no promises but if the books are obtained they will be sent to you; in the meantime I have
felt I must write and explain my silence and the fact that
I had not neglected your request.

I suppose it was thanks to you that I received a little
while ago an announcement of Alfred Perlès book, MY
FRIEND HENRY MILLER. If you are responsible I
am very grateful. I ordered it from London and also
placed an order for your Rimbaud. The Perlès has been
received and has given me infinite pleasure. My only
fault found with it is that it is all too brief. I found it so
good that I wrote a few lines to Perlès to that effect.

A friend of mine in Holland who is a great admirer
of your work has sent me the Signet volume, NIGHTS
OF LOVE AND LAUGHTER.[1] The introduction by
Kenneth Rexroth is excellent. I was particularly interested in his linking of you with Restif. You will remember I suggested this analogy to you in a letter back
in 1947. I can't say I find much in common between you
and Casanova on whom I have been working for two
years. My book, CASANOVIANA,[2] is being printed at the
present time in Austria and I shall send you a copy. It is a
pot-pourri similar to the Restif which I sent you.

Is there any chance of your coming to Europe again in

the near future? It was a source of great regret to me
that I missed you in 1953. I went home a year ago for
three weeks to receive an honorary degree of Doctor of
Humane Letters[3] (why it was given to me I can't explain) but I didn't leave the eastern seaboard.

When is *Nexus* to appear?

I am delighted to see you are being made available to
the American public in pocket books. I hope they will
be a source of income to you. It is certainly time you were
becoming better known in the United States. I have
found it astonishing on a number of occasions to drop
the remark among Americans that "our greatest author
by far is Henry Miller" and to have them exclaim, "I have
never heard of him, who is he?" What a commentary on
how modern American literature is taught in our colleges!

My wife joins me in warm regards to you and your
family.

Cordially yours,
J. Rives Childs

---

[1] [New York]: New American Library, [1955].

[2] *Casanoviana: An Annotated World Bibliography of Jacques
Casanova de Seingalt and of Works concerning Him* (Vienna:
Privately printed for the Casanova Society of Virginia by C. M.
Nebehay, 1956).

[3] Awarded by Randolph-Macon College.

Dear friend –

Returned home a few days ago after three terrible months in N.Y. where I finally buried my mother. Found heaps of c/s [correspondence] to answer. Among them one or two from you which I assume my friend Emil White answered.[1] If there was anything he failed to do, let me know.

Will now finish the "Big Sur" book,[2] whose underlying theme is Paradise.

Often think of you and wonder how you find life in Europe. Wish we could make it over again. But with my mother's death I have been saddled with new problems.

Do you ever meet Michel Simon, the film star? If so, do give him my warmest regards. He was wonderful to me.

All the best meanwhile.

Cordially,
Henry Miller

---

[1] White settled at Big Sur, Calif., soon after Miller. See Henry Miller, *Letters to Anaïs Nin,* ed. G. Stuhlmann (New York: Putnam, 1965), p. 331. White is the editor of *Henry Miller: Between Heaven and Hell* (Big Sur, Calif., Big Sur Publications, 1961).

[2] *Big Sur and the Oranges of Hieronymus Bosch* ([New York]: New Directions, [1957]).

Dear friend Miller:

Thank you so much for your letter of May 3rd. I am
sorry to learn of the loss by you of your mother. You were
fortunate to be near her when her end came. When I lost
my own mother I was in quarantine on an island in the
Red Sea and did not learn of it until five days after she
was buried.

It must have been your friend Emil White who sent me
the four paperbacks which I requested. I did not receive
any bill but I have totalled up the prices marked which
come to $1.95 and have added something for postage
which I hope will cover the cost. Please convey my
thanks to your friend for acting so promptly. I would
have replied sooner but I have been away to Vienna to
look after my book on Casanova which appears next
month and of which you will have a copy. I have also begun work on my memoirs in four volumes, the first to be
entitled UP FROM EARTH'S CENTRE.[1] I sent the mss
of the first volume to an agent in New York who sent it
back and asked me to cut it by one fourth. I expect to
spend the summer trying to do that. The agent also apparently took objection to the frankness of my work. Apparently what the great American public wants are fairy
tales and not anything suggestive of life's realities.

I have recently been giving myself the treat of rereading your works. Nothing finer has been written in recent
years on the South than the tribute you pay it at the end
of THE AIR CONDITIONED NIGHTMARE.[2]

No, I do not know Michel Simon but if I ever run
across him I shall not fail to give him your greetings.

I am sorry to hear there is no immediate prospect of
welcoming you in Europe. I am wedded to France and
can't imagine living anywhere else. After France I think
I like Austria the best. The French are going through a

very trying period but I think they will come out of it in the end. If we would only be a little less ready to tell other people how to run their affairs the others might do a lot better and we would certainly have more friends than we have. The American people, however, are determined to make the world over in the image of the Democratic Party and the Methodist Church and that is no good either for ourselves or for others.

I hope we may soon have your NEXUS.

This conveys to you all the best and the hope we may some day meet somewhere in Europe.

Very cordially yours,
J. Rives Childs

[1] Not yet published.
[2] "The Southland," pp. 283–88.

My dear friend Miller:

I met Thyde Monnier yesterday here in Nice where she
lives. I am not sure you have heard of her as she has
never been translated into English (although in German,
Swedish, Hungarian etc.). I had never heard of her myself until about four or five years ago when I read the
first three volumes of her autobiography, MOI, a fourth
volume of which was published last year.[1]

MOI is a remarkable work, first of all because it is an
autobiography of a woman, of which I believe there are
very few (the only other one I can recall is the very erotic
MÉMOIRES D'UNE CHANTEUSE ALLEMANDE)
and secondly, by reason of its utter sincerity. Mme Monnier, who has been married and divorced twice, began
writing only in late life. She was born in Marseille,
worked for some years as a corset saleswoman, and made
a success of her writing by refusing to be daunted by any
obstacles. In other words she is a woman with infinite
gusto. She has published more than thirty volumes; I have
read only her autobiography.

I had never met her until yesterday and we had a long
talk together. I suspected she would be a great admirer
of yours and when I mentioned your name her face lit
up, enraptured. She showed me those of your works
which she had in French translations (she does not read
English) and told me they were her bedside companions.
When I informed her you and I were in correspondence
she seemed as if she were ready to embrace me in the
thought that I was bringing her closer to you. She ad-
mires you profoundly and showed me a copy of PLEXUS
with her annotations. "If I could only have a short line
from him," she exclaimed to me.

I promised I would write to you and that I felt sure
with your generous nature you would send her a word of

greeting. Her address is Villa L'Oiseau Chanteur, Cimiez, Nice. If you have never read MOI I am certain if you expressed an interest in reading it she would be glad to send you the volumes, or I would be glad to send them to you.

You will be receiving shortly from Vienna my CASANOVIANA which is being printed there these days. I think you will be interested in certain parts of it. You will find your name in the index. Please let me know when you receive it.

I have been working for several years on my autobiography and have recently finished a redraft of the first volume which goes to a New York agent next week. It is called UP FROM EARTH'S CENTRE. It is to be eventually in four volumes if I can find a publisher for the first. I have the feeling you would like parts of it at least.

Is there any early prospect of the appearance of NEXUS?

My wife and I leave here about November 1st on a Danish freighter for Japan and will be in the United States in February. I am still hoping we may meet some time, if not in the United States, perhaps in Nice where you can count always on a warm welcome from Thyde Monnier and me, as well as doubtless many others.

With cordial regards and good wishes,

As ever yours,
J. Rives Childs

---

[1] Vol. I, *Faux départ* (Monaco: Éditions du Rocher, 1949); Vol. II, *La Saison des amours* (1950); Vol. III, *Sur la corde raide* (1951); Vol. IV, *Jetée aux bêtes* (1955). Madame Thyde Monnier died in Nice in 1966.

Dear friend –

Thank you for writing me about Mme Monnier. I will write her, yes. Apparently you haven't yet received a copy I mailed you of "A Devil in Paradise."[1] In the longer work I speak of your work on Restif and quote from your preface.[2] The big book won't be out till next January.

Nexus is shelved for the time being.

Maybe we'll meet here – in Big Sur. No plans for travel thus far.

Good to hear of your work – you're a giant of a worker, I'd say.

By the way – the p.b. will come out in French by Correa – and in 3 instalments (Sept. Oct. Nov.) in Les Lettres Nouvelles (Paris.)[3]

Heat terrific! Must stop.

Ever yours,
Henry Miller

---

[1] [New York]: New American Library, [1956] (paperback).
[2] *Big Sur*, pp. 221–22.
[3] *Un Diable au paradis*, tr. Alex Grall (Paris: Corrêa, 1956).

My dear friend:

Your letter of the 8th reached me this morning and
I am most grateful to you for sending a line to Thyde
Monnier. She is a very remarkable woman. I have written
her that she may expect a line from you and have asked
her to send you volume 1 of MOI and have told her if she
does not have a copy to let me know and I shall try to
find one for you. Of the four volumes only the first two
are really interesting.

A DEVIL IN PARADISE was received by me two
days ago. A few days previous I received from Paris
QUIET DAYS IN CLICHY which you had asked the publishers to send me. I have enjoyed them both enormously
and thank you so much for thinking of me. I feel very
privileged to have the inscribed copy of the first. The enclosed small check will, I hope, serve at least to cover
your out of pocket expenses in sending them. You are
imposed upon enough by your many friends, as I can see
after reading A DEVIL IN PARADISE, and I do not wish
to add to but rather to subtract in my small way from
your burdens.

After reading A DEVIL IN PARADISE my wife remarked: "What a fine person Henry Miller is!"

I have had the visit recently of Marc Chadourne, the
French writer, who is teaching in the United States. He
is working on a biography of Restif de la Bretonne and
he wanted my cooperation.[1] I have urged him to include
in his work some comparison of Restif and yourself and
I think he means to do so. I had hoped to do this study
some time and I may still do so but other projects have
diverted me from it for the time being.

The CASANOVIANA is out and you will have a copy in
a few days. If you do not receive it within a month please
let me know. UP FROM EARTH'S CENTRE has gone

to my agent in New York. This is the best thing I have
ever done and it is something you will like: the story of
my boyhood in Virginia, my college days, my first visit
to France in 1915, my life in the American Army in France
when I headed the Enemy Cipher Bureau,[2] my association with the Peace Conference, the Hoover Mission in the
Balkans, and my work with the Associated Press at the
White House in 1919–1921. It may be too strong meat for
the American public.

We leave here November 1st for Japan and should be in
S.F. either in January or February, depending upon
whether the Canal is open. I shall get in touch with you
on reaching S.F.

I am flattered to hear you made use of my preface to
Restif in your BIG SUR. I shall look forward to reading
it with the utmost pleasure.

With warm regards

Yours ever
J. Rives Childs

---

[1] Marc Chadourne, *Restif de la Bretonne; ou, Le Siècle prophé-
tique* (Paris: Hachette, 1958). Parts of the book were written in
Childs's library at Nice.

[2] See David Kahn, *The Codebreakers* (New York: Macmillan,
1967), pp. 327, 333, 337–39, 348, 355, 361, 1029–36, 1038, 1041,
and 1052 for some of Childs's cipher activities in 1918 in France.

Dear friend –

Very kind of you to send me that check, which I didn't want but accept in spirit offered.

Did you see "Aller Retour N.Y." (French version) pub. by la Guilde du Livre, Lausanne?[1] The preface and post-face (new) will interest you. Have none here or would send.

Henry Miller

---

[1] The first edition, printed at the author's expense, was put out by the Obelisk Press in Paris in 1935 (Siana Series No. 1). The Lausanne edition (1955) was translated by Domique Aury.

Dear friend –

Where is Marc Chadourne to be reached (by letter) now? I have something to ask him, about Melpo Niarchos whom he introduced me to in Hollywood years ago.[1]

Let us know a week or so in advance of your coming. We have no definite plans at the moment – but are always awaiting the miracle that will enable us to go to the orient.

I am very eager to read your autobiog! Did you ever know Nicholas Roosevelt – he is a near neighbor.

New Directions may be writing you for permission to quote from your book. Please leave a forwarding address.

This in haste.
Henry Miller

P.S. I haven't seen "Quiet Days" myself. Don't know when I'll get a copy. Is there any possibility of sending me one or two thru the diplomatic pouch?

---

[1] The lady who was then Mrs. Stavros Niarchos apparently made quite an impression on Miller. The introduction occurred some dozen years earlier than the date of this letter.

My dear friend:

Your postcard of the 18th and letter of the 21st came
this morning.

I had a postcard a few days ago from Marc Chadourne
from the Restif country of Auxerre. I think he is on his
way back to the States. You can reach him at Niles
Hill Road, Waterford, Connecticut. He is teaching French
at Connecticut College in New London.

The French version of "Aller Retour" is down on my
list to order and I am glad you reinforced my intention
to acquire it. I shall write for it today to Switzerland. If
you know of any dealer on the Coast who might happen
to have "The Happy Rock" published by Bern Porter in
1945 and would ask them to send it to me I would be glad
to send a check.[1] Do please put me down for an auto-
graphed copy of "Big Sur" and I shall send you a check
in payment.

I am not sure whether I have ever met Nicholas Roosevelt or not. There is one Roosevelt who was with the
Farmer's Loan and Trust in Paris during the First World
War who figures in my autobiography.[2] The mss went
to Ny on the 11th; it is too soon to have had any news
as to the reaction of my agent.

Please tell New Directions there is no need to write me
for permission to quote from my Restif. I accord it to you
now without reserve and if necessary you can send them
this letter.

If you will write the publishers in Paris to send me
another copy of "Quiet Days" I will bring it to you and if
I can't get to Big Sur I shall mail it from S.F. Unfortunately I can't make use of the diplomatic pouch even for
myself but I shall have no trouble in bringing it.

We are off on November 1st from Marseille. Following my departure you can always write me here and my

mail will be forwarded. You can also write me % American Embassy, Tokyo where I should be towards the end of December and at the St. Francis Hotel in S.F. where I should be about Jan. 20th. I shall get in touch with you upon landing in S.F. If I can do anything for you in the Orient let me know.

With warm regards as always,

Yours ever,
J. Rives Childs

---

[1] *The Happy Rock: A Book about Henry Miller* was printed by the Packard Press, Berkeley, Calif., and offered for sale by Bern Porter in 1945.

[2] Nicholas Roosevelt, the author and conservationist, was Miller's neighbor while he lived at Big Sur.

Dear Rives Childs –

As I wrote your friend Cabot Colville [Coville] the
other day,[1] it's just impossible for me to go to S.F. to meet
you and Mme. Childs, however much I would like to. I
suggested to your friend that I would be able to meet
you in Monterey, if you wished, or happier still if he
could bring you here to our place. It takes about an hour
and a quarter by car, from Monterey, to get here. (No
buses). And there are no trains to Monterey from S.F.
in the morning, if I am correct. Since you only have a
few hours, really, it all seems problematical.

Frankly, I think we should just wait until we can get
together leisurely – either here or in France. These brief
meetings are never very satisfactory. There is no phone
here either – not within ten or twelve miles. And tele-
grams come thru the mail!

Gallimard has just brought out "Les Livres de ma Vie"
and in the Appendix are the 5,000 odd titles (omitted in
American edition) of *"books read."*[2]

Another curious item – was elected a member of The
National Institute of Arts & Letters the other day.[3] How
it happened, I don't know.

The Big Sur book (in which you figure) will be out in
April, say the publishers. Will send you a copy to Nice
soon as I have some.

I do hope you will forgive me – but I truly want a
better meeting, when it does come off.

Ever yours,
Henry Miller

---

[1] Coville is a retired foreign service officer then living near San
Francisco. He greeted Childs and his wife when they arrived in San
Francisco on their return from their world tour in 1957.

² Tr. by Jean Rosenthal.

³ The following is the citation read by Louise Bogan on the occasion of Henry Miller's induction as an Institute member at the joint ceremonial of the American Academy of Arts and Letters and the National Institute of Arts and Letters on May 22, 1957: "Henry Miller, born in New York City in 1891, is the veteran author of many books whose originality and richness of technique are matched by the variety and daring of their subject matter. His boldness of approach and intense curiosity concerning man and nature are unequalled in the prose literature of our time."

Dear Rives Childs,

Just received yours of the 31st March, with check (for which many thanks) and the manuscript. I am trying to read it, but my eyes suffer. Sounds very interesting. Would you mind sending the typescript? Will write more about it then. I am now interested in everything Japanese. Just finished the book by the novelist, Osaragi.[1] Was fascinated, and at times deeply moved. Wonder if there is anything else of his in translation? It's his attitude toward Japan and Japanese that gets me. Reminds me slightly of my own – toward America. Very fine writer too. Restrained, controlled, masterful. Of course I found marvelous what he says about the true, the old type Japanese woman. I quoted Keyserling on Japanese woman in the Big Sur book.[2] (Won't be out till May 22nd now.) Will mail you a new list of books, recordings, etc. soon.

Glad to hear Mme Thyde-Monnier is not angry with me. I just wrote her the other day, explaining how difficult it is for me to find time to read. Things get worse and worse, as far as incoming mail, books, mags, mss. etc. are concerned. And daily visitors. Intrusions, invasions.

Just read a book called "The Third Eye" by a Tibetan – published in England – Secker & Warburg, I think.[3] Found it quite extraordinary.

Will write again soon. Do please send that typescript.

> All the best meanwhile.
> Henry Miller

P.S. Did you get a copy of "Les Livres de ma Vie" from Gallimard? I think I asked them to send you one. It contains in Appendix the list of "books read" – about 5,000 titles. May interest you.
P P.S. My son, Tony, is watching over my shoulder. He says – "Gee, Daddy, how can you write so fast?"

[1] Jiro Osaragi (pseud. of Kiyohiko Nojiri), *Homecoming*, tr. Brewster Horwitz (New York: Knopf, 1955).

[2] Pages 107–8; Miller took the quotation from the second volume of Count Hermann Keyserling, *The Travel Diary of a Philosopher* (New York: Harcourt, Brace, 1925).

[3] T. Lobsang Rampa (pseud.), *The Third Eye: The Autobiography of a Tibetan Lama* (London: Secker and Warburg, 1956). Miller reviewed the book later (Letter 68, note 1).

H. M. to J. R. C., April 22, 1957

Dear Rives Childs,

Your agents sent me the Fuku script to read, which I
did, and returned it promptly.[1] Was amazed that you
allowed your name (as retired Ambassador) to be af-
fixed to the script. Aren't you afraid of kick-backs? As
I see it, they will not be able to sell that story, because of
its frankness and honesty, to any but the sensational
magazines here. ("Playboy" is the best, if one can speak of
good and bad here, of the lot, and pays handsomely!)
But you will writhe to see in what company you will be!
And the photos which will accompany the text.

I enjoyed reading it and admired you for your courage
in revealing some of the weaker aspects of yourself. On
the other hand, I had the feeling that if you had written
it in French it would have come off still better. I don't
know why it is but when one touches on such subjects,
in English, something unnatural creeps in. One gets
sentimental or crude or self-conscious or something – and
this does not happen, it seems to me, when done in the
French language.

I am getting a slew of Japanese books lately, from all
quarters. Nearly every one is excellent. Their contemporary novelists are adept and some show great discipline and mastery. The woman always looms large. Have
you seen a 17th century one called "Five Women Who
Loved Love" by Saikaku,[2] I think it is? Now I am reading up on the geisha. By the time we get there, if ever,
I suppose the geisha will be extinct!

The Big Sur book is out and I will have a copy for you
in a few days now. You will find reference to yourself in
it. Hope you like it!

Do please convey to Madame Thyde Monnier my
deep apologies for not writing her more about her book.
The great trouble is I keep putting off further explora-

tion of the four volumes because I am inundated with books, some of which I *must* read for one reason or another, and I do so always hoping I will find a stretch of ten days in which to devote myself exclusively to her four big tomes. You can't read a book like hers hurriedly or in snatches. Right now I am obliged to read, and am sunk in it, contentedly, "The Fabulous Concubine" by a Dr. Chang who is coming to see me. (Simon & Schuster book).[3] I think you would enjoy it. He has been in diplomatic service, and in strange countries for a scholar, sage, and a Chinese.

All the best meanwhile. Let me know where Fuku appears, won't you? I know there must be such a girl, though you treated the episodes imaginatively. Do you write her? Send me a photo of her, if you have one, will you?

Sincerely,
Henry Miller

[1] This story, which Childs wrote about a woman he met while visiting Japan, has never been published.

[2] Ihara Saikaku, *Five Women Who Loved Love*, tr. W. T. de Bary (Rutland, Vt.: Charles E. Tuttle, 1955).

[3] Hsin-hai Chang's book was published in 1956.

Dear Henry Miller:

I have been holding your letter of April 22nd to answer it properly and now your kind comments about FUKU, contained in your letter of the 28th, arrive to reproach me for my silence. The fact is I have been working my head off, with a French savant, M. Charles Samaran, to have ready for the printers in July the first of a four-volume edition of the Memoirs of Casanova which will be extensively annotated and offer the most complete text ever published. Samaran is doing the notes and I am preparing the text which involves a marriage of the Laforgue, Busoni, and Schütz editions.[1] I should explain that there is a great deal of material in the two last which is not in the first and vice versa. By weaving the three texts together, so far as that is possible, we are obtaining a much more extensive and a much more interesting edition. It is a Herculean labor and I have had to work day and night and put aside practically all my correspondence.

It was a bit inconsiderate on my part to ask you to read FUKU but I thought it might interest you. The story is entirely true, every word of it although I sometimes think it must have been a dream. She was a remarkable girl and got under my skin as few women have. I could actually feel her spirit hovering over me for weeks after I left Japan. I had one letter from her in the United States but only the one. She promised to send me her picture and if she ever does I shall have a copy made and send it to you. I literally had to write the story but I don't think it will ever be published. My agents tell me it has been turned down so far by ESQUIRE, MALE, STAG, CHALLENGE TO MEN, NEW YORKER, HARPERS, TRUE MAN, PLAYBOY, AND CAVALIER. I think I shall have them send it back to me as I have obtained the catharsis I needed which was the reason why I wrote it.

I shall pass your messages on to Madame Monnier. I feel a bit guilty for having imposed her on you but she has such a profound admiration for you and you mean so much to her that I could not resist asking you to write her. Don't let her annoy you, or me either for that matter. You give much too generously of your time to others.

No, I have never received LES LIVRES DE MA VIE. I enclose check for $12 for it and for BIG SUR. And thank you so much for sending me the list of titles of your works available. I have everything now but INTO THE NIGHT LIFE. When I am able to spare $100 I shall send it to you for a copy.

With cordial regards,

Yours ever,
J. Rives Childs

---

[1] Childs's edition of Casanova's *Memoirs* has not yet been published. The Laforgue edition (Leipzig) was issued in 12 volumes, 1826–38, the Paulin-Busoni (Paris) in 10 volumes, 1833–37, and the Schütz (Leipzig) in 12 volumes, 1822–28. M. Samaran is a member of the French Institute, former chief of the French National Archives, medievalist, and man of letters. Of the contemplated edition, Childs reports that he and M. Samaran signed a contract with Garnier Frères, Paris, for an annotated edition of the *Memoirs* in 1956, but they did not conclude work on the extensive annotations until 1967. The original intention had been to use the classic French (Laforgue) text as the basic text for the edition. This plan was discarded in 1960 when Brockhaus in Leipzig announced its intention at last to publish the integral text of the manuscript. This was brought out in 1960–62 by Brockhaus-Plon with excellent but limited notes. The text was published in Italian in 1964–65 by Mondadori, in German in 1964–67 by Propylaen, in Danish in 1963–68 by Reitzel-Thanking and Appel, and in English in 1966[-] by Harcourt, Brace and World. The publication of the manuscript revealed that the Laforgue text is unworthy of serious consideration reflecting as it does in part the inventions of Laforgue rather than the record left by Casanova. Garnier is still endeavoring to reach an agreement for the use of the Brockhaus-Plon text so that an edition with the Childs-Samaran notes can be published. Childs contributed certain notes to the Italian and Danish editions.

Dear J.R.C. –

Sent the 2 books – separately. Also asked Lincoln Schuster (pub.) to send you (from me) "The Fabulous Concubine," which I found just wonderful. Think you will too. More and more astounded by what you say about that story.

All for now,
Henry Miller

Dear friend Henry Miller:

Thank you for the books which arrived and also for
the kind, inscribed dedications. I am now in the midst of
BIG SUR and like it, in fact I like it so well that I am
savoring it slowly rather than gulping it down, in other
words I am applying the French rather than the American technique in the digestion of this hors-d'oeuvre.

I enclose a check for $12.50 for the two MILLER-
GRAUER records.[1] Ben showed up a few days ago and
we had lunch together, wrote you a postcard from LA
BONNE AUBERGE, reputedly one of the best restau-
rants in France but which I think is far from deserving
its reputation. It is expensive, pretentious and loin d'être
fin.

A few weeks ago at our monthly luncheon of the Pro-
peller Club, of which Major General Charles P. Gross
is president, I was walking in with one of his sisters-in-
law, who knows books (which Charlie unfortunately
doesn't) who happened to remark that Charlie
was a boyhood friend of yours. I had to make a speech at
the lunch and I began by saying that we were all devoted
to our beloved president but I had one grave reproach to
make of him and that was that he was gravely lacking in
appreciation of our greatest living American author.
Everyone was waiting for me to disclose the name of the
American I had in mind but I purposely did not in order
to heighten their interest or rather curiosity. Sad to relate
when they crowded around me at the end to learn of
whom I was speaking there were some blank faces when I
informed them that I had reference to Henry Miller.
"Oh you mean the husband of Marylyn," one of the more
intelligent ones (literarily speaking) remarked. "That is
Arthur," I reminded him.   Did I write you I am now en-
gaged with the former chief of the French National

Archives in editing the most complete edition of Casanova's Memoirs which has ever been published? We delivered the first volume of some 1,100 pages last month and will have the second volume ready in a few months. The first volume will appear early next year and I shall see you receive a copy.

That is all for the time being.

The best as always,

Yours ever,
J. Rives Childs

P.S. Your British publishers wrote and asked for permission to print the extract from RESTIF and I told them of course.

JRC

---

[1] "Henry Miller Recalls and Reflects," two 33⅓ R.P.M. long-playing records, ed. Ben Grauer (New York: Riverside Records, 1956).

Dear friend –,

What a surprise, your letter – these strange rencontres.
Did you know Ben Grauer? As for General Charlie – just
flabbergasts me. I remember him so well, as a boy – a
little older than me. Went to visit Felix, his brother, then
a colonel, at Fort Oglethorpe during the Nightmare
trip. Not much in common there, alas.

I mailed you the album of recordings yesterday. Hope
it arrives in good shape.

What happened to your story? Ever place it? Did you
try "Playboy" mag., Chicago?

Did I tell you of the book "Three Geishas" by Kikou
Yamata (John Day, N.Y. 1956). It was published originally in French, but I don't know by whom.[1] The au-
thoress lives in France. Her father was Japanese *consul*
(I believe) at Lyons. Mother French.

Another wonderful book I just read – but I think a copy
was sent you – is "The Fabulous Concubine." Dr. Chang,
wife & daughter came to see me.

Give warm greetings to Thyde-Monnier, please. Have a
guilty conscience owing to inability to get on with her
work – just no time. Frightful, the interruptions and invasions here!

> My best!
> Henry Miller

---

[1] Tr. from the French by Emma Craufurd. The French edition
was *Trois geishas* (Paris: Domat, 1953).

Dear friend Miller:

This letter DOES NOT CALL FOR AN ANSWER. I
have read BIG SUR with great relish and quite appreciate what you have to say about your burdensome correspondence.

By this time you should have received my little booklet
THE CHILDS' ODYSSEY which I hope you liked, particularly as there is a reference therein to you. You will
find in it what I think of the interview of you by Ben
Grauer.[1] I would like to tell you, however, that last Saturday we gathered a few friends together, including Thyde
Monnier, Professor Saurat and his wife (he is a distinguished professor and writer), Vicomte Gautier-Vignal (an
authority on Erasmus), Mme [Crossa-]Reynaud, head of
the local lending library and one of the few women I have
ever met who appreciates Casanova, and Major General
Charles Gross and his wife (he, one of your boyhood
friends). I played the record for them, made a few remarks
about you, and read a few extracts from your works,
amongst others, the last two pages of the COLOSSUS, the
Sarlat episode in AIR-CONDITIONED NIGHTMARE,[2]
and had at the same time an exhibition of the many works
of yours in English and French I possess. It was topped off
by a few very appreciative remarks by Charlie Gross, to
whom I [am] devoted, about his recollections of you as a
boy. Charlie's remarks were so good I regretted I did not
have them tape-recorded. I have insisted he write them
out. Don't know whether he will.

The object of this letter is to tell you all this and to
say that upon a review of the works of yours I possess
I find that I am lacking the following:

WHAT ARE YOU GOING TO DO ABOUT ALF?,
Porter, 1944
(I thought I had a copy and I may have but I can't
lay my hands on it.)

DAYS OF LOVE AND HUNGER, New Directions, 1955
COLOSSUS OF MAROUSSI, Penguin edition, 1950
CITY OF LOVE, Dell, 1955
ECHOLALIA, Porter
VARDA, Porter
MILLER ET L'AMOUR, Correa, Paris, 1947
H. Miller, Moore, 1943[3]

If you have any of these or all of them which are for sale will you send me what you have with your bill and I will be delighted to send a check. There is no hurry as my wife and I are leaving for India on January 12th for three months and will not be back until the end of April. However, if you send the books and send me a postcard telling me what I owe you it (the postcard) will be forwarded and I shall send you a check at once wherever I may be.

I am hoping the first volume of our CASANOVA will be out early next year (one of four volumes) but we are somewhat dismayed by the report which has come to us that Brockhaus is at last publishing the original text. I am off to Paris on Dec. 26th to find out how we stand. All the best and be assured of a warm welcome if you ever get to Nice.

Yours ever,
J. Rives Childs

[1] Until the death of his wife, Childs states that he "sent out for some years a Xmas letter in the form of a printed brochure giving news of ourselves and of our travels." *Childs' Odyssey* V contains an ardent account of impressions derived from a visit to Japan in 1957. In one place Childs advised his readers to buy the Miller-Grauer recording. He had been "lifted out of myself after hearing it; something of the same effect produced by seeing the Buddha of Kamakura." He ended his eulogy with the phrase, "End unpaid ad." Both Miller and Grauer had excerpts of Childs's praise printed on a card for distribution.

[2] Pages 69–75.

[3] Apparently Childs did not succeed in obtaining several of these

items as they are not listed in the check list of the collection he gave to Randolph-Macon College (see Appendix II). Those missing are *What Are You Going to Do about Alf?* in either the 1935 Paris edition printed at the author's expense or the American edition done by the Knoxville Press, Knoxville, Tenn., and offered for sale in Berkeley, Calif., by Bern Porter in 1944; *City of Love,* an anthology of stories by many writers edited by Daniel Talbot which contains Miller's "Mademoiselle Claude"; *Echolalia,* a collection of reproductions of water colors printed by James J. Gillick and offered for sale in Berkeley, Calif., by Bern Porter in 1945; *Varda: The Master Builder* (Berkeley, Calif.: George Leite, Circle Editions, 1947), reprinted in *Remember to Remember;* Georges Villa, *Miller et l'amour;* and Nicholas Moore, *Henry Miller* (Wigginton, Eng.: Opus Press, 1943).

By *Days of Love and Hunger* Childs seems to mean *Nights of Love and Laughter,* which is in the Randolph-Macon collection. *The Colossus of Maroussi* appears in the Colt Press edition (San Francisco, 1941) rather than in the Penguin edition mentioned here.

60 *Avondale Estates, Georgia; December 20, 1957* ♈

Dear Charlie and Ella,

This address should be reversed but Ella is not too interested in Henry Miller.[1] – Just a day after the receipt of your letter, we had one from Pete telling us of some of his travels in Japan. On one occasion he went to the Kanda section of Tokyo – noted for its numerous book stores. I quote "I found the most numerous bookshops in the whole world I'm sure. I spent hours reading a bit of Henry Miller, just a bit – "

The graduation class picture is on its way. Henry Miller – front row – third from the left – indicated by a small arrow. Ambassador Childs can have a copy made from this of any desired size.[2]

Through the years we have noted mention of Henry Miller – in various magazines – book reviews – The writer – as we recall – was never in accord with what Henry Miller had to say. Neither of us ever had sufficient curiosity to find out what it was all about.

While we were living in Club Drive – and we believe before our country entered the war – 1940–1941 (It may have been later) we had a call from Henry Miller one evening. He and a male companion were staying for the night at an auto court on Moreland Ave. I *believe* I went there to get them – that I returned them to this auto court I am certain.

Henry Miller and his companion spent about two hours with us – Henry doing most of the talking. We – both of us[–] thought he was odd – perhaps because he spoke of matters of no interest to us. He was pleasant looking – easily recognizable from his boyhood picture. Neither he nor his companion were well dressed – downright seedy.

Edith remembers him as a classmate – just an ordinary boy – nothing outstanding. After graduation (February '05) she does not recall seeing him – doesn't know where he went to school.

As you know his family lived on Decatur St. toward Bushwick Ave. – on our side of the street. I can picture his mother – a pleasant blond haired woman – taller than most – and his sister Loretta who appeared to have some nervous affliction. His father I do not recall.

This perhaps is less about Henry Miller and his family than you expected – but as we remember them – they were just ordinary people – like ourselves – who behaved themselves and kept out of trouble.

Henry Miller's rise to fame has come about in such fashion that we were never really aware of it.

We are anticipating a noisy Christmas surely for the gang is going to be here on Christmas morning.

Our love to you,
Edith and Felix [Gross]

[1] Charles Gross, having met Childs and heard him proclaim Miller the "greatest living American author," became curious to recall whatever he could about his boyhood acquaintance. He wrote to his brother Felix regarding Miller and received this reply, which he gave to Childs. Ella Gross is Charles's wife. Edith Gross, Felix's wife, is Miller's coeval.

[2] Charles Gross sent the picture of the February, 1905, graduation class at P.S. 85, Brooklyn, to Childs with his letter of March 20, 1958. For a reproduction of the photograph with a note by Charles Gross on the back, see plate following p. 122.

118 *E. and F. Gross to C. and E. Gross, Dec. 20, 1957*

Dear Rives Childs –

I think $3.25 covers what you owe me – any time. Somehow I mislaid your "Odyssey" – never did get to read what you wrote about the records.

Am writing Charley Gross to-day.

Bon Voyage!
Henry Miller

Dear Charley Gross –

For you are still "Charley" to me after all the years!
Amazing that about fifty years after we last met I should
hear from J. Rives Childs that you, Ben Grauer and he
were at table together. What must have been a bore was
listening to him read from my work! (I've never met him,
you know.)

You must smile when he relates, as I suppose he did, that
there is a resemblance between me and the famous (or
notorious) Restif de la Bretonne!

However —— it was awfully good to know you are still
alive and active, and living in that delightful part of the
world. (Aren't you a neighbor of Cocteau and Maugham?)

I remember you so well. You as a young man – in your
late teens. Very tall, *serious,* earnest – with a very musical
soft voice. Childs says you remember *me.* That's more sur-
prising, as I was your junior by several years and played
no part in your life. (To *us* you and Felix were like fa-
vored sons – of the gods.) But I remember one incident –
do you? – when you threw an old X'mas tree over the
fence – at the vacant lot, corner of Bushwick Avenue –
and it fell on my head and suddenly I was drenched in
blood. I always remember this because I never felt a thing!

If Edith is still with you – I remember her most vividly
– please give her my warm greetings. Or did she marry
Felix? Forgive me if I am mixed up.

My one desire now is to see Japan, Burma, Java. With
two kids – nine and twelve – it's not so easy.

Well, enough! All good wishes to you both.

Henry Miller

P.S. Did I seem "different" from the other kids on the
block then? – that's what I don't know. Later, in my twen-
ties I *know* I was – and paid the price for it.

63 *Roquebrune–Cap Martin, France; March 20, 1958*

Dear Henry,

It warmed my heart to get so friendly a letter from you in response to Rives Childs' tale of my presence at his 'Henry Miller Afternoon.'[1]

Childs, a retired ambassador, with former stations in the Near East and Tangier, is your most ardent admirer. To him you are America's greatest man of letters. He has a complete collection of your works with many first editions and a miscellaneous file, where even the merest reference to you is embraced. Imagine then his horror when he heard that I, after having answered a letter from you some six years ago, had thrown it away. My sister-in-law, Lottie Hubach, in our day a little girl on Schaeffer St, had betrayed me in conversing on their favorite subject. As soon as he could get the floor, Childs expressed his great disappointment in me and launched into a eulogy of Henry Miller. In my shame I did feel grateful to the several members (It was a club luncheon) who, looking confused, audibly whispered, "Henry Miller? Who is he?" – just too ignorant to be withered by his disdain. But the fact that I had known you as a boy redeemed me to grace. Rives invited me to his literary afternoon.

On this occasion Childs played Ben Grauer's records, read several passages from your works, displayed all your books and then asked me to tell what I knew of you as a boy. His audience was mainly French and almost as enthusiastic as he. Keenly attentive to Childs and to Grauer, Gross's meager recital couldn't overcome the pull to the Scotch and soda on the table.

You ask, "Did I seem different from the other kids on the block then?" The burden of my talk was that you didn't.

I told of a boy some three years younger than I with whom I had not been too intimate because of this age spread, but with whom I had occasional pleasant conversations as I passed down the street on my way home from high school, and later, Cornell. I described Decatur Street as no locale for dead end kids; spoke of the German-American inheritance that both of us and so many of our companions had, of earnest, orderly people in modest circumstances. I described you as a clean, attractive looking blond, friendly, alert and eager, after contact had been made, but more inclined to shyness than to dominant leadership. I even expressed the doubt that you had ever kissed a girl before you were 17 or 18. How wrong I may have been I of course, don't know. Unfortunately I did not recall having heaved a Christmas tree on your head with the gory results you relate. (My brain fibres, however, are slowly stretching out to each other and are producing a dim recollection of it.) I did tell of P.S. No 85, of the fine teachers we had in Mr Winter and Dr Perry, whom we have known all of our lives. Your gift for English and interest in writing I felt may have been inspired by the able teachers of Boys' High (Mitchell, Fairley, Hartwell, Butterick) altho I am not sure you attended that high school. Your tall, fair mother, your blond sister, Loretta, your sober, dignified (to us) and well dressed father formed the solid family, typical of those from which most of the friends of my youth, some of them lifelong, had sprung.

My knowledge of you came to a sudden end. There was a great gap in time before I heard of the man. No bridge carried me over from the boy I had known, I had to confess, to the man they were talking about. I could not reconcile the two. I had to assume that the development in that interval was so unusual, indeed, so revolutionary, as to be more a series of explosions than a transition, and that from violent reactions a great writer was born.

Forgive me if my account offends your sense of the real truth, but I had to feed the hungry. I was violating, of course, the sage advice of the first sergeant to the recruit: "Keep your mouth shut, your bowels open and never volunteer."

Le Ha Fleuri
Roquebrune- Cap Martin, A.M.
March 20, 1958

Dear Rives

Here is Henry Miller's graduation picture from Public School
No. 85 at Covert St. and Evergreen Ave. Brooklyn, N.Y.   (Feb. 1905)

"Dear Eighty Five we'll ever strive
To honor thy fair name
We shall by creed, by word and deed,   } Chorus
Our loyalty acclaim."   of School Song
                                          (He also had a
                                          creed, noble but now
                                          forgotten.)

Henry is third from left in the first row
My sister-in-law Edith Thompson (Gross) is third from right in 2nd row.
The Miller, Thompson and Gross families all lived on Decatur St. between
Bushwick and Evergreen Aves two blocks away from the school.
I sent Henry Miller a smaller copy of this picture.

                                          Charley Gross

While in Atlanta with Edith and Felix this last summer, we were speaking of you, of your visit to them just before World War II. Edith brought out your graduation picture (P.S. 85, Feb 1905). I of course, had to have it copied for my friend, Childs. He will be delighted with it when he returns in late April from a winter in India and Burma. I am here enclosing a small copy for you.

You mention your great desire to visit Japan, Burma and Java with your two youngsters. Childs last year made a trip around the world which he recounts in the little book I enclose. His remarks on Japan may interest you. Note also his 'unpaid ad' of you on pages 13 and 14.

Just a little of myself. I married Ella Hubach, an 85 girl. We have five children and fourteen grandchildren – true products of our early environment. Perhaps because we have qualified, possibly, for our protection, we linger on on the Riviera. After some 4½ years with the Army and State Department in Germany I retired in 1952 and have been on the way home ever since. But life is so agreeable here that we float along avoiding a decision to return. But before we crack up we must locate in the States not too far from an Army hospital nor too distant from a National Cemetery.

It was good to hear from you, Henry

My best
Charley [Gross].

[1] This letter is taken from a handwritten copy sent to Childs by Gross.

Dear Rives Childs –

I wrote Charley Gross and just had a good reply from him. He tells me you collect about every thing of mine you can lay hands on.

I wonder therefore if I sent you "Trend," which carries a "preface" I wrote for Sydney Omarr's book – (not yet published) called "The Astrology of Henry Miller"? or the plaquette "The Hour of Man"?[1]

The Signet pocket people will bring out another pocket book of miscellaneous essays & stories shortly. The "Colossus" comes out this month in a paper back edition – $1.25. Then also "The Red Notebook" – see enclosed.[2]

Gross sent me your "Odyssey" which I had mislaid and I found the "free ad" on the albums. Very touched by what you wrote. The album is selling steadily – to my surprise. I suppose you sent Ben Grauer a copy, no?

The Verlag der Arche – Zurich – bringing out soon a book (of mine) of their own concoction, with a number of reproductions of various things and photos.[3] Sounds interesting.

Do you keep all the translations of my work too?

Am still hoping to get to Japan, but don't quite see how to make it yet. Give warm greetings to Thyde-Monnier and ask her to forgive me. I get only about ½ hr. a day for reading now. Am painting quite a bit. Have gallery in N.Y. Will show in Jerusalem soon.[4] All the best!

Henry Miller

---

[1] "A Great Writer Talks about Astrology" appeared first in Sidney Omarr, *1958 Guidebook to Astrology* (Los Angeles: Trend Books, 1958), then in Omarr's book *Henry Miller, His World of Urania* (Hollywood, Calif., 9th House Publishing Co., 1960). The *plaquette* is an offprint of the essay, which appeared in the *Chicago Review*, Vol. X (Autumn-Winter, 1956).

[2] The Signet book is *The Intimate Henry Miller* ([New York]: New American Library, [1959]). The paperback edition of *Colossus* was published by New Directions. An inscribed copy of *The Red Notebook* ([Highlands, N.C.: Jonathan Williams, 1958]) was sent to Childs at the same time as this letter.

[3] *Von der Unmoral der Moral,* selections translated by Oswalt von Nostitz, Alexander Korval, and Ursula von Wiese, appeared in 1958.

[4] Miller's water colors were shown at the Jerusalem Artists' House in 1958.

Dear Charley –

Forgive brevity of this – am swamped at moment. So good to get all the news. I do remember Ella Hubach! But I went to Eastern District High not the other you mention. Happy too to get '85 photo and the Childs' Odyssey which I had lost.

I think Childs confounds my earlier experiences on Driggs Ave. (14th Ward, B'klyn) with the Decatur "Street of Sorrows" ones.

In 1953 my wife and I spent a month in the house belonging to Michel Simon (cinema actor) at La Ciotât. The coast there reminded me a little of Big Sur.

Warm greetings!
Henry

Dear Rives Childs,

Did I tell you that I had a letter from Charley Gross and that he sent me a copy of your "Odyssey"?* Reading this account I was impressed by your reaction to Japan, which is my own feeling about the country and the people – without having been there. It is the one country I want to visit – and before too long. (Did you ever look up "Trois Geishas" by Kikou Yamata?) Do!

Charley tells me that you have quite a collection of things by and about me. Perhaps I can add to it from time to time. Do you want magazines in which texts of mine appear? (By separate mail I am sending you photostatic copies from the card files at U.C.L.A. – not complete – which list the magazines in which texts by or about me have appeared. I have no use for it.) I also enclose with this "the suggestions for correction of French version of "When I Reach for my Revolver" – and the carbon of that text, in English.[1] Think you would like this. The Library has the many pages of suggested corrections I made for the Swiss-French translator when he was doing my Rimbaud opus. This aspect – my French! – may be unknown to you. With this I also send copies of letters to the Oslo attorney about the trial of "Sexus" which is still not decided, the judge having fallen ill.

Should you know of any one who would care to purchase of me some corrected texts – and this isn't meant, please believe, as a hint to you to offer me a price! – please let me know. I have big blocks of the first draft of the "Big Sur" book and a number of "prefaces" and so on. Prefaces: I wonder if you have many of these; I seem to have done a dozen or more for various writers – recently one for Durrell's "Black Book"[2] which his publishers promise to bring out after the Justine tetralogy. And did I ever send you the book-mag. called "Trend," with my preface (on astrology) to Sydney OMarr's unpublished ms. "The Astrology of Henry Miller"? There are so many little items I believe you would like to have. Well, there is time.

(Do you have the little text – "The Hour of Man"?)

Incidentally, when I think I can make it to Japan – and I believe I would take my wife and the two children, who are 9 and 12 now – do you think I could get a free passage, by boat or air, for writing something? I have a _____ publisher named Tanaka who lives in Kamakura – in a big modern house, I hear, who has invited me to stay if I ever come – but I doubt I would. And I have an old friend from the days when I took "boarders" who is still alive, in Tokyo. My desire is two-fold; to meet a genuine Zen master (an anonymous one preferably) and a genuine geisha. And – to see that Kamakura Buddha, of which I have often seen photos.

Enough! Good cheer!
Henry Miller

---

* That "free ad" for the recordings – I can't get over it. Either I or Grauer will make use of it! [Miller's note.]

¹ Actually Miller sent Childs a typescript of "When I Reach for My Revolver" containing revisions on the text in pencil and ink, a list of sixty suggestions for corrections to the French text which had appeared in *Synthèses* (Brussels), No. 97 (June, 1954) under the title "Quand je saisis mon revolver," and, finally, a fair copy in typescript of the essay. First published in English in Fernando Puma, ed., *Seven Arts*, No. 3 (Indian Hills, Colo.: Falcon's Wing Press, 1955), the essay has been reprinted in *Hummingbird*.

² Miller's Preface has not yet appeared with Lawrence Durrell's *The Black Book*, which was first published by the Obelisk Press in Paris in 1938. But see Miller's Preface in Durrell's *Justine*, tr. Roger Giroux (Paris: Corrêa, 1960), Miller's "The Durrell of the Black Book Days" in Harry T. Moore, ed., *The World of Lawrence Durrell* (Carbondale, Ill.: Southern Illinois Press, 1961), and Miller's "Letter to Lawrence Durrell" in Durrell, Miller, and Alfred Perlès, *Art and Outrage* (London: Putnam, 1959; New York: Dutton, 1961).

Dear Rives Childs –

If you have copies left of your "Odyssey" send me all you can spare, won't you? Can make good use of them. Several batches of mail coming to you – when I can get mail out. We are temporarily marooned by huge slides. Rains have been heavy – and not over yet.

Henry Miller

DON'T WASTE YOUR VALUABLE TIME TO ANSWER THIS

Dear Henry Miller:

I am most grateful for the various brochures you have been good enough to send me. I think I had better list them:

1958 Guidebook to Astrology
Span, issue no. 2
New Statesman, 29 March 1958
The Hour of Man
Review of THE THIRD EYE
Review of QUEST
Reproduction of my little ad of your recording[1]

I would have acknowledged them sooner but I have been pushing myself to finish the manuscript on which I have been working for some eight years which I have entitled tentatively OF MANY A VANISHED SCENE.[2] Now that I have finished it I am far from satisfied and think I will have to do it over once more. The trouble is it is two books: an autobiography and the historical background of events in the Near East where I served for thirty years. Our mutual friend, Marc Chadourne, who is spending a few days here is now reading it and I hope to profit from his comments.

A few days ago I had the visit of a childhood friend from Lynchburg, Virginia. I spoke about you to her a couple of years ago and although she is a great reader she was one of that great group of American illiterates who had never heard of your name. She inquired of a student at Washington and Lee University in Lexington, where she lives, if he knew where she could get any of your books. According to her account he looked at her aghast and whispered that the University Library possessed one of your works but that it was kept under lock and key. She finally found BIG SUR but she was left puzzled by the reaction of the student. I read her a few paragraphs of your tribute to the Southland in NIGHTMARE and then I read her what I regard as among your finest pages, the description of your visit to Sarlat, from the same work. She was absolutely spell-bound.

I saw Thyde Monnier some days ago and gave her your message which she much appreciated. She quite understands that you cannot attend to your work and answer all the letters you receive. She is happy to have a small place in your heart.

I tried to interest PANAM in a free passage for you to Japan. The reply came back that the request would have to be made on the part of your publishers and that, in such circumstances, it would be given consideration but that they made it a rule not to deal directly with writers. Perhaps you can get New Directions to take it up; I am sorry not to have succeeded.

One other item. I loaned your record to a charming American woman who is a poetess. She returned it with a note stating she had been deeply impressed and that you had helped her find the solution to one of her problems.[3] So you see, the ripples from Big Sur extend to the Riviera.

All the best to you. You have a host of friends here who would welcome you with open arms whenever the spirit moves you to pass this way.

J. Rives Childs

[1] The articles from *Span* and the *New Statesman* were Rudolph Steiner's "Henry Miller – A Debt," *Span* (New York), No. 2, 1958, and Herbert Read's "As the Grass Grows," the *Statesman*'s review of *Big Sur*. Miller's reviews were "A Review of *The Third Eye* by T. Lobsang Rampa," *New York Review*, Spring, 1958, and "Quest," a

review of George Dibbern's *Quest* in *Circle Magazine* (Berkeley, Calif.), No. 8 (1946).

² A new title for the unpublished autobiography formerly called "Up from Earth's Centre."

³ Mrs. Evan Potter, who still lives in France.

My dear friend Miller,

I have seen in the papers that you will be a member of the American jury at the Cannes Festival. Is it possible that I shall at long last have the pleasure of meeting you after the correspondence we have had these last thirteen or fourteen years?

I am asking Dr. Jean-Etienne Jouve, of the Festival, to pass this letter to you.[1] The purpose of it is to extend you a most hearty welcome to the Coast and to express the hope that you and your wife, together with Dr. and Mme Jouve come to Nice at your convenience sometime during the Festival and have lunch with us here (I am sure Dr. and Mrs. Jouve would be glad to bring you). The simplest would be to fix on a date with them and then telephone me some morning when I am always in. Or I would be glad to meet you if you come by train.

Curiously enough, I was so taken with the article about you which you had the editors send me from Paris[2] (which I acknowledged both to them and to you, mentioning Dr. Jouve's name) that I dashed off an article about you which a London magazine is printing in October and of which you will have a copy in due course.[3] I think it will amuse you.

I shall be sending also to you this autumn a biography of Casanova which Rowohlt in Hamburg is having translated into German (I am negotiating for its publication in English) and which will also probably be translated into Italian and published by Mondadori.[4] In the meantime warm regards,

Yours ever,
J. Rives Childs

[1] Dr. Jouve was the founder in 1959–60 of the Comité d'organisation du cinema sur la côte d'Azur.

[2] Karl Shapiro, "The Greatest Living Author," *Two Cities,* Dec. 15, 1959.

[3] "Collecting Henry Miller."

[4] *Giacomo Casanova de Seingalt, in Selbstzengnissen und Bildo-kumenten,* tr. Hans-Heinrich Wellmann (Hamburg: Rowohlt, 1960); *La vita incredible e vera di un mago, di un furfonte, di un avventuriero protagonista del suo secolo, Casanova,* tr. Biagio Lon-goni (Milan: Area Editore, 1961).

Dear AMBASSADOR –

Just read your touching text in "The Private Library" (thanks to Ben Grauer).[1] Here I am in Germany – since 3 months. Soon to Paris, then South. Hope to see you in Nice before winter is over. The Tropics are coming out shortly – in Hebrew, in Italian, in Spanish, and in Dutch – and in America by the Grove Press, N.Y.[2] (But keep this under your hat, please!)

Warm greetings!

Henry Miller

[1] This letter or note appears as an inscription in a copy of a German pamphlet sent to Childs by Miller. The pamphlet was Henry Miller, *Ein Weihnachtsabend in der Villa Seurat,* tr. Renate Gerhardt (Hamburg: Rowohlt, 1960), a section from *Remember to Remember.*

[2] Available data on these foreign editions follow: *Hugo shel sarton* ("Tropic of Cancer"), tr. Ednah Kornfeld (2 v.; Tel-Aviv: Desheh, 1962); *Tropico de cancro* [e] *Tropico del capricorno,* tr. Luciano Bianciardi (Milan: Feltrinelli, 1962); *Tropico de Capricornio,* tr. Mario Guillermo Iglesias (Buenos Aires: Editorial Rueda, 1962); *De Kreeftskeerkring* ("Tropic of Cancer"), tr. John Vandenbergh (The Hague: De Bezige Bij, 1962).

Dear J. Rives Childs,

   Many thanks for copy of The Private Library, which
has been forwarded to me from my previous address.

   I have read with particular interest your article on Collecting Henry Miller etc. and was surprised to learn that
you had discovered H.M. as far back as 1939 when he
was still comparatively unknown. The fact that you already then sensed his importance as a writer is all the
more astonishing as few critics at the time mentioned him
at all and fewer still had a word of intelligent praise for
him. And what makes me feel quite especially good is
the knowledge that a man of your high official standing
(American Ambassador – no less!) should have had the
unorthodox courage to distribute copies of Tropic of
Capricorn among friends!

   Thanking you again for sending me this copy,

Yours very sincerely,
Alfred Perlès

P.S. I wonder whether you ever did meet H.M. since
your return from Japan, in 1956. I was staying with him
at Big Sur at that time, but we've met several times since
– in Paris, in spring '59, and later in the south of France
(with the Durrells), and again last year in Rome at
Easter. He happens to be in Germany now (Hamburg)
but plans to go to Paris shortly, then down south to Pro-
vence: which might be a convenient point for you to link
up with him at last!

A.P.

Dear friend Miller,

Thank you for your charming note of Feb. 6th inscribed
on the Rowohlt pamphlet which I found upon my return
from three weeks in Austria yesterday.

I also found a letter from Alfred Perlès acknowledging
a copy of the article about you which I had sent him. In
his letter he told me that you were in Hamburg, that you
planned to go to Paris shortly and then in this direction.

Not knowing you were in Europe I sent you a copy of
the article to Big Sur (the one Ben Grauer forwarded
you) and I am glad you liked it. The PLA people[1] wrote
and asked me for an article on Restif. I replied that I
would prefer to do one on you and when they expressed
an interest I sat down and dashed it off in about an hour.
I have a few copies left and if there are any persons you
would like me to forward it to I would be glad to do so.
Perhaps to Durrell whose address I do not have?

Ask Dr. Kusenberg for a copy of my GIACOMO
CASANOVA which Rowohlt published last October.
Allen & Unwin are bringing out a much more extended
edition entitled CASANOVA, A BIOGRAPHY BASED
ON NEW DOCUMENTS in May and there will be a
French translation to be published by Pauvert. Scribners
is now studying the possibility of an American edition.[2]

If you come this way do let me know as I was disappointed at not meeting you when you were in Cannes.
My telephone number is _____. I may be going to
Paris on March 5th for two days to see Pauvert. It would
be fun to have lunch or dinner with you there in one of
your old haunts.

I have been working intermittently on my memoirs for
some years but my feeling is there are too many and I
can't get them into the shape I like. Every kitchen maid
is writing her memoirs these days.

When is volume II of NEXUS to appear?[3] I have only
the first volume in English.

All the best. Do let us contrive to meet somewhere
some time.

Yours ever,

J. Rives Childs

[1] The Private Libraries Association of Great Britain, of which
Childs was elected the first American president in 1965.

[2] Dr. Kurt Kusenberg is the editor of Rowohlt's Monographien
series, which includes Walter Schmiele's biography, *Henry Miller in
Selbstzengnissen und Bildokumenten* ([Hamburg]: Rowohlt,
[1961]), as well as Childs's Casanova biography. Although highly
praised in Europe and soon to be published in Japan, Childs's
Casanova biography has still not been published in the United
States.

[3] Not published yet (1968).

Dear Mr. Childs,

I am writing you for Henry Miller, who at this moment is very hard at work finishing up a play which has kept him busy for the past few weeks.[1] Henry says to offer his apologies for not writing you personally. I am sure you will be hearing from him just as soon as he gets a breathing spell.

Henry will be leaving Reinbek shortly and going first to southern Switzerland for a time. After that his plans are still indefinite but he hopes to get to Cannes and meet you one day soon. (Sorry, *Nice,* not Cannes!)

In answer to yours of 23 Feb., Henry enjoyed your P.L.A. article very much indeed and he would be pleased if you could send a few copies of it to him at Agence Hoffman, 77 Boul. St-Michel, Paris 5°.

Henry still hasn't written Volume II of *Nexus* but hopes to get around to it soon.

> Very cordially yours,
> Vincent Birge
> (FOR HENRY MILLER)

---

[1] *Just Wild about Harry: A Melo-Melo in Seven Scenes* [Norfolk, Conn.]: New Directions, [1963]).

Dear friend –

    I expect to arrive in Nice by car, with my companion
in arms, Vincent Birge, April 1ˢᵗ or 2ⁿᵈ. Please leave word
at American Express if you are in town. This time we
must meet. Have been on the road 3 weeks or so.

Henry Miller

Dear friend Henry,

My wife and I were both delighted to have news of
you in your kind letter of the 5th. I am sorry, however, to
learn that before leaving you were unable to find anything that responds to your mood where you might have
been tempted to settle near us.

Last Sunday was a red-letter day in our calendar.[1] As I
told you, I had misgivings lately about meeting you face
to face. I think there are singularly few writers who live
up to the expectations we form of them from their books.
It is with no intention of flattering you when I repeat that
you did much more than that. We found your conversation the living embodiment of all that you write.

There is precious little good conversation here on the
Riviera; for me Sunday was one of the most memorable
days of my sojourn of eight years here – in fact, the most
memorable. What a pity we didn't have a tape recorder;
it was all pure Henry Miller. My wife and I were not the
only ones made happy by your visit; my maître d'hôtel,
Robert Roby, was deeply touched by your kindness in
dedicating for him one of your books, PLEXUS. And I
was even more moved when I read after your departure
the inimitable records you left of your visit in the dedications to those of my Miller treasures which you signed.[2]

I saw Charlie Gross and his wife yesterday and they
were most interested in the news that I gave them of you.
I explained that you came in unexpectedly and that you
did not have the time to look them up. They were genuinely disappointed not to see you.

I had a letter from Pauvert yesterday agreeing to the
translator I desired for the translation of my CASANOVA
from English into French. I have written Dr. Kusenberg,
enclosing the photo[3] I showed you and telling him we
both thought he might be interested in having it for the

monograph on you.[4] It is most gratifying to one who has recognized your worth these twenty-one years that you are at long last obtaining the appreciation which you so richly deserve.

Let me urge you not to dissipate your energies in writing me under any sense of obligation. Our rapport, is such, I feel, that we are able to communicate through the still mysterious ways of a world intelligence, of which we know as yet little except that they are open to those who make themselves receptive.

My wife joins in every good wish to you and Mr. Birge. Come again and soon!

Very cordially,
J. Rives Childs

[1] Miller, accompanied by Birge, spent most of the day with Childs and his wife in their apartment in Nice on Easter Sunday, 1961. M. Matarasso, a bookdealer in Nice, had informed Childs on Saturday that Miller was in town looking for him, and Childs met Miller at Queenie's, a water-front cafe. Miller agreed to have lunch with Childs and his wife in town and to spend the afternoon in the Childs's apartment the next day. As Childs recounts it, "We talked and talked. Verbal pyrotechnics. Miller would laugh a great deal. At peace with the world. Nothing could ruffle him. Talked exactly as he writes, rhapsodically. His eyes filled with wonder and envy when I talked about my travels. Exclaimed his envy frequently. I don't know when I've ever had such a talkfest. We flitted like a lot of bees from one flower to another. My wife was as spellbound as I was. Miller's humanity, his humor, were absolutely contagious. I thought of Mark Twain, or better still, Rabelais. A real love of the world. For Miller a good hearty laugh is as much an antidote to troubles as anything in the world. I tried to sum up the meeting later, but it was like trying to describe a magnificent sunset. Something that couldn't be reproduced. From a spiritual point of view it was one of the richest days I've ever known. Not the slightest suggestion of affectation about Miller. Transparent honesty, genuineness. His spiritual integrity was striking. I felt better after talking to him than after most sermons I've heard. An inspired quality in Miller. He is an Innocent."

[2] That Childs was still moved when he wrote the letter may be inferred from the unusual number of typing errors (here corrected) in this letter.

[3] The school photograph sent by Gross.

[4] Schmiele's biography.

Montpellier (Hérault), France;
                    April 12, 1961 ♈

Dear friend –

Thank you for your very warm letter! I mailed you
to-day some texts, including two typescripts. The one,
"My Life as an Echo," I wrote for my Italian editor,
Feltrinelli. It will appear in Italian and probably in German too, by Rowohlt Verlag. The other, "The Humming
Bird," may appear in "Esquire" next year.[1] They want
exclusive rights – first showing. (*Sic.*) Anyway, please
don't offer either of these to any one for publication anywhere, I beg you.

I discovered here one item you may not have – a text
of mine about my trip to Spain in 1953 – "Mejores No
Hay" – which has thus far appeared only in French, in
the Belgian revue "Synthèses."[*2] The owner and editor of
the revue is Maurice Lambilliotte, a wonderful man, who
is one of the ministers (of mines, or something) in the
Belgian government. Maybe you know him.

My friend Durrell gets back from London this week-
end. I'll probably stay on here all this week and next. I
must find a place soon – even if only for the Summer. My
children plan to join me soon as school is out. But where
to look? I feel really discouraged. Nothing seems to suit
me at present.

I'm sorry too about not meeting Charlie Gross and his
wife. It may yet happen, tell him. I do hope to see you
and Madame Childs too somewhere sometime again before too long.

Must stop. All the best meanwhile.

                                  Henry Miller

* published probably 5 or 6 years ago – ?? Don't have a copy.
[Miller's note.]

[1] The manuscript for "My Life as Echo" is an eight-page typescript. It was published in the collection *Prefazione ai Tropici,* ed. Valerio Riva (Milan: Feltrinelli, 1962), and later reprinted in *Hummingbird.* The manuscript for "Stand Still like the Hummingbird" is a photocopy 15 pages long. It was published in *Esquire,* Vol. LVI (Nov., 1961), and reprinted in *Hummingbird.*

[2] No. 100 (Sept., 1954).

Dear friend Henry Miller,

You overwhelm me with your bountiful attentions. I
did not reply at once to your kind letter of the 12th until
I had received the texts you were thoughtful enough to
send. I have read them at once with the same compelling
interest with which I read all that you write; you may be
sure that they will not be revealed.

I wish I could aid you in finding a suitable place to
settle, if only for the summer. Friends are no more to be
relied on in these matters, however, than in the choice
of a wife. If you would care for me to look and tell me
about what you are seeking I will be glad to try.

Charlie Gross and his wife were genuinely disappointed at not seeing you. I explained that we had met à
l'improviste and had no time to get in touch with him.
I would be deceitful if I said that Charlie admired what
you write; as a soldier he is not much of a reader but he
does admire what you have achieved. His wife's two
sisters who went to school with you were here a couple of
years ago and we had no end of fun in ribbing Charlie
about his abysmal ignorance of you as a writer. They
attended a luncheon group of which I was then [later]
the president and I seized the occasion to announce that
I had been discussing America's greatest writer with
Charlie and Ella Gross' sisters and gave the assembly the
chance to guess who the writer was, emphasizing that he
was far from having gained in his own country the appreciation accorded him outside those shores. Of course,
the guesses made were so wide of the mark that in the
end I had to reveal your name. You will not be surprised
that at the conclusion of the luncheon there were some
who came up and interrogated me: "Who is Henry Miller?" What a commentary on us as a nation!

Two weeks ago today you were with us and the spirit

of your pulsing personality still enshrouds us. Whenever you are in this vicinity just walk in and make yourself at home. Don't stand on conventions and wait for an invitation; consider us as members of your family of humanity whom your writings and spirit have touched and moved deeply and have been made one with you.

Don't bother to answer this letter; we have no need of standing on ceremony with one another. It will be answered in your heart in any case and that is what matters.

All the best as always,

J. Rives Childs

Dear friend –

I received the two issues to-day here.[1] Thank you. Durrell is still in London. I'll hang on till Saturday.

We covered the region you suggested.[2] Yes, it was quite remarkable – but not the place for me. I seem unable to make up my mind about anything these days. Continually depressed and baffled and blocked.

For the few hours that I was with you and Madame Childs I was lifted. It was like an injection. But once on the road again my sombre, dull, despairing mood returns. It's "astrological," I do believe.

I'll write again later, from somewhere. Meanwhile all my best. It was a great day chez vous. Stay well!

Sincerely,
Henry Miller

[1] Perhaps Miller is referring to Childs's article, "Collecting Henry Miller." He had earlier requested additional copies.

[2] During the visit at Easter, Childs recommended Cagnes, the country above Vence, and the region between Grasse and Draguignan.

Dear friend –

Here's another to add to your ever-growing collection.[1]

Henry Miller

Off to Ireland now.
ERIN GO BRAGH!

[1] This note to Childs is inscribed in a copy of Schmiele's book on Miller.

Dear friends –

Just got your good letter here in Pacific Palisades (Calif.) Leaving Aug. 15ᵗʰ for Edinburgh Festival and then the Continent.

Wonderful to hear about your college project.[1] Much doing here now. Hope I do see you and Madame Childs soon again. Always remember you –

Henry Miller

---

[1] Childs was invited to be Scholar-in-Residence at Randolph-Macon College for the spring of 1962. He gave the address on the occasion of the formal opening of the Walter Hines Page Library. Under the title of *The Rewards of Book Collecting*, the text was printed for distribution to alumni and friends of the College.

Dear friend HM,

You will recall that I wrote you from Florida about the talk I gave at Randolph-Macon College on May 30th which concerned you in part. As was to be expected it proved to be the part of most interest to the audience and has had some curious repercussions, amongst others an editorial in the Lynchburg NEWS, my home town, of which I enclose a copy. The editorial writer is a friend of mine which explains the altogether undeserved references to me. What is important are the references TO YOU.[1]

It is immensely gratifying that in a town as conservative as Lynchburg Phil Scruggs should have had the courage to come out with so strong an affirmative vote in favor of HM. It must have shook the city fathers.

I hope you received a copy of my address THE RE-WARDS OF BOOK COLLECTING which was sent to you some weeks ago to Big Sur from the Librarian of R-M College at Ashland.

A few days ago Thyde Monnier, the French writer, to whom you wrote several years ago at my request and whom you made happy for the rest of her life in so doing, telephoned me to say she had read in CANDIDE that you had been in Edinburgh and had headed for southern France. She wanted to know if she might look forward to seeing you in Nice and I assured her that if you did show up I would do my best to arrange a meeting. She would not only be flattered but would enter into a seventh heaven of delight to meet you face to face.

If you do get down this way do let me have a postcard from you to that effect so that you may come and spend one if not more days with us. I may be driving to Bourgogne for about five days about October 10th but otherwise I shall be here and it would give both my wife and

me the greatest pleasure to receive you and to take up
again the threads of our talk which we left off on Easter
Day 1961.

Cordially yours,
J. Rives Childs

[1] The editorial by Philip Lightfoot Scruggs appeared Sept. 7,
1962. The references to Miller occurred in the following paragraph:
"An authority on Jacques Casanova, and on Restif de la Bretonne, he
[Childs] also is among that select and distinguished group of strong
admirers of the American writer, Henry Miller, and in his comments
justly makes laughable and hypocritical those bitter critics of Miller
who have so nearly created in the public mind the idea that Miller is
an obscene writer, or deliberate perpetrator of obscenity. What Mr.
Childs said would be above their heads, but to truly literate readers
he will make such appeal as to compel them to read Miller and
discover for themselves that he is a great writer."

J. R. C. to H. M., September 22, 1962

Dear friend –

Just got your letter here, by Hildegard Knef, where I am staying a few days, then on to Berlin to see about the production of my play at the Schiller Theater this winter.[1] Have just returned from short trip to Austria – where I found every thing just ducky. Marvelous countryside.

No, I haven't yet received the "address" you gave. Will come eventually.

I was only the other day looking at one of Thyde-Monnier's books (in German) in a bookshop in Starnberg. Got quite a thrill. Do tell her! And give her warm regards.

I don't know when I will get to your vicinity again. One day, however – not too late, I hope. Now we live on velvet, we septuagenarians!

Yes, very good to see Herr Scrugg's comments in a Virginia paper. Progress, what!

Capricorn is now out in the States.[2] Don't know yet with what results. I shall probably be back in California in November.

Meanwhile my very best to you and to Madame Childs whom I remember vividly.

Let us keep in touch!

Ever yours,
Henry Miller

---

[1] *Harry* was not produced at the Schiller Theater because Miller would not agree to make a number of changes in the play.

[2] The Grove Press, New York, published *Tropic of Cancer* in 1961 and *Tropic of Capricorn* in 1962.

Dear friend Henry Miller,

It has been an infernally long time since I had any news of you except through the HM News Letter[1] and no one seems to be able to inform me where you are. I had Pauvert send you in care of the address you gave me on the Bd St Michel a copy of my CASANOVA translated into French but have had no acknowledgment.

This letter is to tell you that and also to inform you what infinite pleasure your correspondance with Durrell gave me. I was so taken with it that I wrote George Wickes at once and urged him to proceed with further volumes before we had all passed into the great beyond.[2]

My wife and I sail next Sunday from Havre for NY where we shall be until the 9th. I wrote Ben Grauer for the new records you had made with him and he answered that there was no time to send them before my departure but that I could pick them up when I passed through.[3] We go first to Oxford, Ohio where I am to give a lecture on April 11th and then to Ashland, Va., where I am to be in residence at R-M College and give four lectures. Incidentally I sent you a copy of the one I made there last year, part of which was devoted to you, which earned encomiums in the Virginia press.

On May 23rd I shall be in Chicago to talk with a publisher about a new book and we go thence by train to San Francisco to embark on the S.S.MARIPOSA of the Matson Line on May 26th, stopping at Bora Bora, Tahiti, Rarotonga (don't you like the names?), then to New Zealand for three weeks, to Australia for another three and back here from Sidney by the S.S.GALILEO of the L[l]oyd Triestino, via Djakarta, Singapore etc. Back here at the end of August.

If this reaches you in time let me have at least a post-

card % R-M College, Ashland, Va., where we shall be
until about May 20th.

I think I shall save time by mailing this in NY City.

Cordially yours,

J. Rives Childs

P.S. I have also obtained and read JUST WILD ABOUT
HARRY. It is good, very good but I think (although I
know nothing of dramatic art) that it would have been
more satisfying if you had brought in the prostitute at the
end, if even through just a line or two.

---

[1] *The Henry Miller Literary Society Newsletter* was published by
Edward P. Schwartz and Thomas H. Moore at 121 N. 7th Street,
Minneapolis, Minnesota. *The International Henry Miller Letter* is
published irregularly by Henk van Gelre at Fransestraat 5, Nijmegen, Netherlands.

[2] George Wickes, ed., *Lawrence Durrell and Henry Miller: A
Private Correspondence* (New York: Dutton, 1963).

[3] Henry Miller, "Life As I See It," one 33⅓ R.P.M. long-playing
record, ed. Ben Grauer (New York: Offbeat Records, 1962).

Dear Rives Childs –

Just got yours of March 25th. I am in new quarters, as you see[1] – with my two children. Aside from a touch of sciatica (very painful) I'm fine. Been painting rather than writing. Did 75 w.c's in last 3 months. The play will be given at Edinburgh Festival – by the Cambridge Players – and probably in Spoleto too (this July.)[2] Yes, it has its weaknesses, I know. But I hope to do better next time.

Your itinerary, as usual, sounds fascinating. I am due in Paris end of May to assist in producing film of "Cancer" there – may be 17 weeks.[3] Won't have a chance to travel about.

I did get your Casanova – but have still to read it. Books pour in on me like rain – and requests for Prefaces, etc. Never was busier. It's almost too much. I need a secretary – or two.

Did you hear of "success" of *Cancer* in England?[4] What a surprise! I wish I *could* see you in S.F., but I know in advance it will be impossible. If you ever get down this far, do come see us. (Telephone is _____ – Pacific Palisades.)

My daughter will go to college next term – doesn't know where yet. I wanted her to work for me instead but she wants a fling at college first. Too bad – it's so useless, *education.*

Well, I must stop. So many letters to write daily – une vraie corvée. I got a great kick recently when my girl, Val, came home with Rimbaud's poem – *Romans* (?) – to translate. Never thought to see that day. The boy, Tony, is also taking French now – and does quite well.

Well, all the best! Drop me a post card from some exotic place, eh? And warm greetings to Mrs. Childs!

Henry Miller

[1] Against the printed letterhead Miller had written "new home!"

[2] The world premiere of *Harry* was held July 7, 1963, at the Theatro Caio Melisso in Spoleto. On order of the Lord Chamberlain the curtain was rung down on the second night of the production in Edinburgh on grounds of obscenity.

[3] "Tropic of Cancer will be made as a motion picture according to information from California. Newsletter informants say that Bernie Wolfe, now doing film treatment on *Playboy* will handle the writing chores. Wolfe is best known for his collaboration with Mezz Mezzrow in the book, *Really the Blues.* . . . Embassy films president Joseph Levine announced purchase of the book Dec. 15, 1962. Production will probably start early next Summer in France" (*Henry Miller Literary Society Newsletter,* No. 11 [Dec., 1962]). The film has not yet been produced (1968).

[4] *Tropic of Cancer* (London: John Calder, 1963).

Dear friend Henry Miller,

It was a joy to receive your letter of the 26th with the interesting enclosure but you should not have taken the trouble; a postcard would have sufficed. Whenever I receive a letter from you I feel like a thief who has stolen precious time from you.

Ben Grauer in New York gave me much news of you on my arrival. He is sending me the new record he has produced and when I return to Nice I shall loan it to the Nice Radio to whom I made available your first to their great delight.

Your letter of the 26th was most useful also. When I spoke here last year I awakened or rather stimulated an interest in you which I found still aflame upon my return this month. The wife of one of the professors,[1] who was working on a paper on me, decided to discard it and substitute one on you, which I think evidenced great judgment on her part. She has been pumping me for material and I took the liberty of showing her your letter which she found most helpful. As a result of my talk last year the Librarian has purchased all your works available. This will be supplemented by my bequest of my own collection (first editions of all your works with the exception of TROPIC OF CANCER and ALLER RE- TOUR for which I am still searching) so that the Library here will eventually have the most complete and exten- sive collection probably of any library in the east.

I am glad to hear you did receive my CASANOVA which had a very good reception in France. Madeleine Chapsal of EXPRESS came down to Nice to interview me when it came out. The greatest encomium she could pay me in her article was to remark that "the writer is a friend of Henry Miller." It reminded me of a charming article Theophile Gautier once wrote about one of his acquaintances who aspired to literary recognition. When the friend died the greatest tribute his associates felt that they could pay him was to inscribe on his tombstone: HE LOVED SHAKESPEARE.[2] Perhaps they will put on the slab above my grave: HE WAS A FRIEND OF HENRY MILLER.

My ship the S.S.Mariposa will dock in Los Angeles (I presume, San Pedro) on the morning of May 27th. I don't know whether we shall be leaving port later in the morning or in the afternoon. If not until the afternoon and you are still in Pacific Palisades and it would not be too great an interruption, perhaps you would join my wife and me on board for lunch. In any case I shall telephone you at the number you gave me on our arrival and if you are there we can at least exchange a few words.

It would give us the greatest pleasure if you paid us another visit in Nice. We could put you up for as long as you would care to remain and you could make Nice your headquarters and come and go as you liked. We shall be back on August 26th.

My wife joins me in most cordial regards and every good wish.

J. Rives Childs

[1] Mrs. William Stanford Webb, wife of the chairman of the English Department at Randolph-Macon College.
[2] See Letter 21, note 2.

Dear good friend –

I am not at all certain I will still be here May 27th –
and, even if I were, it would be hard to get to your ship
at San Pedro.

Better just call me on phone – yes? (_____) I expect to be in Paris from June to October.

On se verra quelque part!

Henry Miller

Dear Rives Childs –

Your Odyssey of 1963 only reached me here a few days ago. After reading it I am inclined to agree with your good wife Georgina. "No more!" This last one must have been devastating. The new world to explore, it seems to me, is Africa, China, India, Indonesia. Certainly not Australia, New Zealand, Canada – or the U.S.A.!¹

There is so much to tell you that naturally I can't do it – in one letter. Lots has happened. Lots of changes. *Etc.* My daughter (18) is getting married next month. My boy (15) goes to a private school – a military academy – next week.

I think the play ("Harry") is just about to get recognition – first off in Scandinavia, then Germany, then Italy. Here last, naturally. I'm on a new one – a one act play – pure burlesque. (But no music or dancing this time.)²

It's quite possible I will get to Europe some time this Spring. If I do, I hope to look you up. The film project for "Cancer" is going through all sorts of litigation at present. New film projects are in the air. The "Smile" will definitely be given by the Hamburg Staatsoper in 1965 – early. The *opera*, I mean – which I believe is *very good.*³

I did a lot of painting last year – aquarelles – and will probably continue this year. I wish I could do this exclusively.

I recently read several books by Laurence Van Der Post and found them wonderful. Do you know him – from South Africa?⁴

And last night I picked up Marie Corelli's "The Life Everlasting."⁵ Must say I have a great respect for her. Have read a number of her "occult" novels in the past. She gives me a wonderful lift. (Does this astonish you?)

Enough now. All my best ever to you and to Georgina.

Do your future voyaging at home – it's more rewarding!

Henry Miller

P.S. Give greetings, please, to Thyde-Monnier. Had beautiful letter from her which I shall answer soon. Always snowed under with c/s.

P.S. Also interested again (deeply) in the life of Alexander the Great. Just reread Heinrich Mann's "Alexander" – not a good book but has some remarkable passages – especially anent Clitus, his friend.[6]

---

[1] Commenting on their recent journey around the world – from France to the United States and thence through the islands of the Pacific to Australia and New Zealand, Burma, Indonesia, India, Egypt, and back to France through Italy – Mrs. Childs said, "No more long trips." Since Childs's retirement in 1953 they had traveled a great deal, covering in their journeys much of the Far East, Mexico and South America, and Africa.

This letter is written on stationery which carries, in addition to the name and address at the top, an italic line in quotation marks: "The time of the hyena is upon us."

[2] *Harry* has not yet (1968) been performed in Scandinavia. The new play has not been published (1968).

[3] The opera, based on Miller's *The Smile at the Foot of the Ladder* (New York: Duell, Sloan & Pearce, [1948]), was written by the Triestino composer, Antonio Bibalo. It was produced at the Hamburg Staatsoper in April, 1965.

[4] Laurens Van der Post, the well-known explorer and travel-adventure writer, has published a number of books: *Venture to the Interior* (1951), *The Dark Eye in Africa* (1955), *The Lost World of the Kalahari* (1958), and *The Heart of the Hunter* (1961), all done by Morrow in New York.

[5] *The Life Everlasting: A Reality of Romance* (New York: George H. Doran, 1911).

[6] No information available.

H. M. to J. R. C., January 24, 1964

Dear friend Henry Miller,

Your letter of the 24th gave me no end of joy. I had
been thinking of you a great deal recently, dipping into
your works as I do whenever I want a lift and reading,
and savoring slowly, George Wickes' HENRY MILLER
AND THE CRITICS which I had ordered and had received a couple of weeks ago.[1] I had been tempted to
write you to learn how you were and whether you had
any plans to come this way and then my eye fell on your
"Draconian Postscript":

> "The greater part of the day is taken up by the thou-
> sand and one imbeciles who, for a variety of reasons
> and in a thousand devious ways, intrude upon my
> privacy."[2]

I decided that, while I was sure you did not count me
among the "thousand and one imbeciles," or the thousand
and two, I should refrain from imposing upon you and
addressing a letter to you which, in your conscientious
way, you might feel called for a reply. Now that you have
taken the initiative I am going to less [let] myself go,
while emphasizing that I do not expect a reply and that I
shall only take up the little time for you to read this.

Nothing in life has given me any greater personal satis-
faction than the recognition increasingly accorded you
and I rejoice with you in your success as much as if it
were my own. I shall always be supremely grateful to
that British clerk in Brentanos to whom I appealed, when
rushing in to catch a train in 1939, "for some books in the
style of Joyce" and who handed me a fourth edition of
TROPIC OF CANCER, firsts of BLACK SPRING and
MAX and a first of Durrell's BLACK BOOK. The result
was an enrichment of my life for which I shall be eter-
nally grateful both to that clerk and to you. Eight or nine
years ago, when addressing an American club luncheon,

and introducing Charlie Gross' sister as a school friend of "the greatest living American writer" I offered to wager that there was no one in the audience who could identify whom I had in mind. No one could. Then when I gave your name everyone looked perfectly blank. Of course there has been a great change since then.

When Madeleine Chapsal wrote a very good review of my CASANOVA in *L'Express* the greatest compliment she thought she could pay me – and I agreed with her – was that "he is a friend of Henry Miller." It reminded me of the story that Theophile Gautier tells of a French writer in his literary circle who never emerged from obscurity by his writing. When he died his friends considered what epitaph might appropriately be placed on his headstone. Finally, they had carved HE LOVED SHAKESPEARE.[3] Perhaps my greatest title to remembrance may be that "he was a friend of Miller and recognized his genius from an early date."

I am delighted to hear that there is a possibility that you may come to Europe this Spring. We are going to spend a few weeks quietly in England and Scotland in May and June and in August I am thinking of going to Budapest, Warsaw, Prague and Berlin. I am not asking or expecting that you answer this letter but I do hope you will let me know when you come to Europe. As you know we have a small apartment but we would be delighted to have you come and stay with us. I could turn over my bedroom to you and move in with my wife where there are two double beds and you could come and go as you like. You would be as free to do as you pleased as if you were in your own home. And perhaps you might decide to make the trip with me to the Iron Curtain countries. I am going otherwise alone as my wife, who is Russian, has no desire to penetrate that particular curtain.

I have just sent to America, to Henry Regnery in Chicago to be exact, an autobiography I have been working on for ten years. Their literary editor took the pains to offer me pages of suggested corrections from which I greatly profited; in fact it is the only one of my works with which an editor has taken so much trouble. The result pleases me very much. The last time I saw their editor I told him I didn't understand why they were wasting so much time with me as I didn't think the manuscript was worth it. I do, however, now. In the final chapter there is a good deal about you, of how I first discovered you, of my letter to the *Revue de Paris* complaining of their false estimate of you, of how we entered into correspondence as a result and of your visit to us on Easter Day, 1962 [1961]. Grow, the editor, liked this part very much. He was as surprised, as Perlès had expressed himself to me in a letter, that my knowledge and appreciation of your work went back to 1939.

Not long ago I read a remarkable eulogy of your correspondence with Durrell in *Le Monde* by Jacqueline Piatte. I could not resist writing and congratulating her on it. It was by far the best notice of that work I had seen. I also wrote George Wickes when it appeared and told him it was no use promising us more after the lapse of years when I, for one would be dead, and that he should get on with the continuance of it. I noticed that even *Time*, which never loses an opportunity to sneer, was impressed, as, I think, have been all those who read it.⁴

I have chattered along quite enough and have already more than abused your time.

Let's have another meeting this year. Most cordial greetings as always from Georgina and me.

J. R. C.

P.S. I failed to answer one or two of your questions. Yes, I know Van der Post's books and find them first-rate. I met Marie Corelli at Stratford in 1918, in fact I had tea with her. Her companion told us this story of her while we were awaiting her appearance. A visitor asked a taxi driver conducting him to her home whether she had ever married. The driver snorted. "Sir, don't you know that Shakespeare has been dead for more than 300 years?" She was so devoted to Shakespeare that she had moved to Stratford to make her home there. I am ashamed to say I have never read her. I am, however, as interested as you in the occult. I could give you some astonishing instances from my own experiences which I should write up some day. There is a subject we could spend some days on!

[1] Carbondale, Ill.: Southern Illinois University Press, [1964].
[2] *Ibid.*, p. 189.
[3] One of Childs's favorite anecdotes: see Letters 21, 34, and 85.
[4] The review in *Le Monde* appeared on Nov. 2, 1963; the review in *Time* in the issue of March 1, 1963.

Dear good friend –

I have been in bed three weeks – just recovering now. Meanwhile came your "In Memoriam,"[1] which I am going to read this evening. I didn't know your wife had died, or I would have written you sooner.

Soon I must go to the hospital for an operation on my hip – osteoarthritis. Later I should go to Paris (June or July) to assist in filming "Tropic of Cancer."

I haven't done much writing but quite a bit of painting – water colors. Are you up to date on new books of mine? Recently I put in order all the translations of my work – over 100 books. Cancer is now out in Norwegian, Slovene, Russian (printed in U.S. – Grove Press). Must be about 17 or 18 foreign editions of *Cancer*. Curious, what! There is a beautiful *German* edition of my play – with one of my w.c's as jacket.[2]

My friend Joe Gray wants to be remembered to you. He is very grateful for the reception you gave him in Nice last year.[3]

How goes your life now? What do you do these days?

I write you to Virginia, not sure where you are.

If there are any books of mine I can send you, do let me know. Did you see the last one – "Henry Miller on Writing" (New Directions?)[4]

Must stop now. Get tired very easily. Expect to be in good shape again in a week or two – ready for the surgeon's knife, so to speak.

I do think of you often, even if I don't write. My mail gets bigger and bigger, alas! I'd like to "abdicate" – and just paint.

My very best ever.
Henry Miller

[1] J. Rives Childs, *In Memoriam: Georgina de Brylkine Childs* (privately printed, 1964). Mrs. Childs died unexpectedly in Nice November 23, 1964.

[2] Further information on these three foreign translations of *Cancer* is not available. The play appeared as *Ganz Wild auf Harry* (Berlin: Gerhardt Verlag, 1963).

[3] Childs remembers the visit: "I don't recall when it was in 1963 that I had a telephone call from a young American who introduced himself as Joe Gray, of California, and stated that Henry Miller had suggested that he call on me. I invited him to come out and he showed up shortly thereafter. He stated that he was making a study of Arthur Rimbaud and that he was particularly anxious to meet Monsieur Henri Matarasso in Nice who had a valuable collection of Rimbaud material. I telephoned Matarasso and made an appointment to accompany Gray to his villa where we were received that same day, as I recall, and where M. Matarasso very kindly exhibited some of his many treasures, I acting as interpreter. It struck me as curious that Gray should be making a study of a French poet when he was unable to speak or read French with any ease. Gray left either that day or the day following and I never heard what became of his project."

[4] Edited by Thomas H. Moore and published by New Directions in 1964.

My dear friend Henry,

It was good of you to write me in your kind letter of
February 25th to acknowledge receipt of the memorial to
my wife. She was a great admirer of yours and we spoke
so often of the happy Easter which we spent together
with you in our home, often expressing the hope that you
would pay us a return visit and linger longer.

It is most distressing to know that you have not been in
good health and that you are awaiting an operation on
your hip. May everything turn out well in order that you
may have many more years of creative work. It is a con-
stant joy to me when I read in so many publications of
the recognition that has come to you.

I have not gone in for the translations of your works
except for the French. So far as those published in English are concerned I think I have everything except the
last volume published by New Directions, HENRY MIL-
LER ON WRITING. It is most kind of you to offer to
send it to me but I am ordering it, as an author can only
be truly complimented by the purchase of his produc-
tions. Merle Miller has a charming observation on this
subject in his GAY AND MELANCHOLY SOUND,[1] a
masterly work, far superior to most of his writing.

I left Virginia the middle of last month to return here
to put my affairs in some order. I had dinner in NY with
Ben Grauer and Melanie and we spoke, naturally, of you.
I had lunch with my literary agent who is peddling, so
far without success, my BETWEEN TWO WORLDS.[2]
Regnery kept it for a year but finally concluded that it
would not be commercially profitable. I think they are
probably right. I am still working on an annotated edition of Casanova's MEMOIRES for Garnier in Paris and
we hope to finish next year.

Between now and June I shall do a lot of traveling with

a Eurailpass to Vienna, Scandinavia and Paris, as I love trains. I shall settle down here for the summer and late in October I go to Randolph-Macon College for three months as Visiting Scholar – a pretentious name to cover a very modest function.

Give my regards to Joe Gray whom it was a pleasure to meet. If you come to Paris this summer drop down here where you will always find a room in my apartment and we can go where you like in my car. All you have to do is to let me know a few days in advance.

My very warm regards and don't bother to acknowledge this. I understand your correspondence problem; mine is small in comparison with yours but I spend a couple of hours every morning dealing with it. I go to London in May to address a British society of bibliophiles of which I have been elected president for 1965 and in September I have promised to participate in a symposium on Casanova in Milan, organized by the Italians and French there.

Yours ever,
J. Rives Childs

P.S. Excuse the typewriter but my handwriting gets shakier and shakier.

---

[1] New York: W. Sloane Associates, 1961.

[2] Between his retirement in 1953 and 1968 Childs worked intermittently on an autobiography entitled successively "Up from Earth's Centre," "Of Many a Vanished Scene" and "Between Two Worlds." As early as 1958 he had expressed dissatisfaction with it (see p. 130). In 1967 he subjected it to a thorough revision in the interest of greater homogeneity. Reentitled "Farewell to Foreign Service: Thirty Years in the Near East" it is scheduled for publication in 1969 by the University Press of Virginia.

Dear friend Henry Miller,

I am Scholar in Residence at Randolph-Macon College for several months this winter and commute between Richmond and Ashland.[1]

Another purpose of my presence in Ashland is to arrange for the proper housing of my library which I am presenting the College, including my collection of your works of which, in first editions, I lack only that of the TROPIC OF CANCER. I am also trying to persuade the College, of which my great grandfather was a founder and president of the board for its first 44 years, to establish a College Press.

It happens that I have about fifty letters from you since we began our correspondence about twenty years ago and it has been suggested that the Randolph-Macon College Press would dash off to a flying start if it published as its first book the letters I have from you.

I am writing to seek your consent and to assure you that if the plan materializes we would see that you had the opportunity to look over a typescript of the correspondence before it was printed. Your literary agent would doubtless have ideas about the royalties to which you would be entitled as it is far from my idea to profit personally from this venture; nor would such be the intention of this College.*

Do let me have your comments and also a word as to how you are as it has been some time since I heard from you.

With warm regards, and hoping that our Easter meeting of some years ago may some day be repeated, believe me

Cordially yours,
J. Rives Childs

* The oldest Methodist College in America! [Childs's note.]

¹ The original of this letter is in the collection of Miller material at the University Library of the University of California, Los Angeles. It is printed here through the courtesy of the Department of Special Collections of that library.

Dear Rives Childs,

What a great pleasure to hear from you again! Of course you have my permission to publish the letters, providing of course I have a chance to see them before going to print – I mean in galleys – in order to eliminate anything I think may offend some one. The terms can be easily arranged between us. I have no literary agent here in America, only in France, for foreign publications.

This December 26th I will be 74, and except for an arthritic hip and an irregular heart, am in good shape. I ride my bike every day and swim when the weather permits – in a heated pool, to be sure.

There is so much to tell you that I wouldn't know where to begin. Perhaps the greatest pleasure I have had in recent times is to see the translations of my books – in about 17 languages now, with "Cancer" the most often translated, which includes Russian (a Grove Press edition) and Croatian (Yugoslav gov't press), and one little book in Polish (The Smile).[1] In all there are now over a hundred translations of all my books. This is about the only real thrill I can say I have experienced in connection with my work.

As for magazine articles, by and about me, there is no end to them. I enclose one which was done in Italian – thought you might like for your collection. Also enclose a pamphlet about Antonio Bibalo, who composed an opera based on my "Smile at Foot of Ladder." There is a possibility now that the San Francisco Opera Co. may be interested in it.[2]

The film of "Cancer" is still hanging fire. Should commence filming, in Paris, next Spring – but one never knows.

I just finished a 15 pages Introduction to a new de luxe edition of George Grosz' "Ecce Homo," which the Grove

Press, N.Y. will bring out in the Spring.[3] Between times I continue to make water colors, and have hopes now of getting a new album of colored reproductions (perhaps 40 of them) published in the near future. I am enclosing some new run offs (post cards) taken from "To Paint is to Love Again."[4]

Well, this will have to do as a starter. I am glad to see that you are active and take it for granted that you will enjoy being a scholar in residence at that old Methodist College. If you are a Methodist, then I suppose I am a Baptist!

Meanwhile all the very best to you, and do have a good holiday season. Myself I observe no holidays any more. They are meaningless to me.

Sincerely,
Henry Miller

P.S. Are you acquainted with the writings of Isaac Bashevis Singer, the Yiddish writer? I adore his books, and feel closer to him than to any American writer.

---

[1] There have been two Yugoslav translations of *Tropic of Cancer*. One in Croatian, *Rakova Obratnica,* appeared in Rijeka in 1967 and one in Slovene, *Rakov Povratnik,* in Ljubljana in 1964. The Polish translation of *The Smile at the Foot of the Ladder, Usmiech u Stop Drabiny* was published by Państwowy Instytut Wydawniczy in Warsaw in 1964.

[2] Henry Miller, "Anche a New York, ci sono i poveri," *Epoca* (Milan), Vol. II (Feb. 3, 1951). The Bibalo pamphlet is a brochure printed for Wilhelm Hansen Musik Forlag in Copenhagen, publishers of the opera in 1962. The opera has not yet (1968) been performed in San Francisco.

[3] Published in 1966.

[4] Henry Miller, *To Paint Is to Love Again* (Alhambra, Calif.: Cambria Books, [1960]).

Appendixes

Collecting Henry Miller: or, What Miller Means to Me

By J. Rives Childs

Henry Miller, the despised and rejected, seems at last to be coming into his own. In the December number of *Two Cities,* Karl Shapiro calls him the greatest of living writers. As such an evaluation implies a knowledge of world literature which few of us possess I would be less categoric. I have long claimed that he is the greatest of living American authors and it was immensely gratifying to me when Lawrence Durrell, a far more competent critic than I, recently voiced such an opinion.[1]

Few writers have been more misunderstood than Miller. In 1947 when M. Thiebaut, the eminent editor of the *Revue de Paris,* wrote slightingly of Miller, I took issue with him. As my letter offers a summary of views I still hold I quote it in part:

It has been particularly interesting to me to find in your study of recent trends in American literature the linking of the names of Restif de la Bretonne and Henry Miller. Unfortunately you do not pursue the comparison. . . . Henry Miller, of course, is a lineal descendant of Restif in the family of literature; their origins, careers and literary output offer interesting affinities, a study of which, it is hoped, will some day be undertaken. Both men were born into a world in a profound state of political, social and economic upheaval; both found themselves early in a state of rebellion against the societies in which they were born. Both beat their wings against what they regarded as the insanities of the times.

A gross injustice is done in my opinion in attributing a pornographic purpose to the work of either of these two writers.

[1] Reprinted from *Private Library,* III (Oct., 1960) 34–37, by permission of the Private Libraries Association of Great Britain.

I look upon the licence of language used by Restif and Miller as a means chosen by them to express their profound dissatisfaction with the world about them. Far from pornographic, their language is to be regarded as a means used by them to shock an insensible world into an awareness of the insane organization of society. Both Restif and Miller are profoundly humanitarian. The world to them appears a madhouse; to attract the attention of the inmates one must shock them. That at any rate is how I read Restif and Miller. To state that "dans le championnat international de la pornographie, il est certain que Miller se classe bon premier" is to reveal a complete misconception of Miller. It is as unfair to judge Miller on the basis of certain passages in certain of his works as to form a judgment of Restif on the basis of *Anti-Justine*.

You also fail, it seems, to understand the irony of Miller, an irony in the great tradition of Swift. When Swift proposed as a means of relieving the distress in Ireland to offer 100,000 Irish children for human consumption many of his contemporaries took him seriously. Similarly you appear to have taken seriously Miller's injunction, " 'Hommes, achetez un fusil et tuez-vous l'un l'autre.' Surtout ne travaillez pas. 'Il vaut mieux tuer les autres que gagner sa vie.' "

What Miller is doing here is to sum up what he considers to be the prevailing spirit of the times. There is doubtless also the thought in the back of his mind that, considering the present state of the world, mankind would do well to make a good job of killing each other. To infer, however, that this is his philosophy of life is as wide of the mark as to ascribe the acceptance of cannibalism to Swift.[2]

I thought Miller might be interested in my letter and I sent him a copy, thus initiating a correspondence which has continued to this day. In his reply he referred me to his *Obscenity and the Law of Reflection* as representing the best summary of his views on the so-called pornography in his work. He was particularly impressed by the affinity I had drawn between Restif and himself and

---

[2] The passage from Childs's letter to Thiébaut has been rephrased somewhat.

asked me to send him something of that author's work. The next time I went to Paris I picked up a one-volume modern edition of the *Nuits de Paris* which I sent him. When he published *Books I Have Read* he made passing reference to Restif as well as to me as 'an American attaché in Jidda.' I enjoyed one of the heartiest laughs I had had in weeks; it happened that I was, in fact, American Ambassador to Saudi Arabia but I had kept it carefully concealed from Miller. With the knowledge I had gained of him I feared that once he found out the character of my position it might put a damper on our correspondence. Later in his *Big Sur* he devoted several pages to our correspondence and to Restif. By that time I was identified as 'American Minister.' Happily it never altered our relationship.

I had discovered Miller as early as 1939 through one of the happiest chances in all my book-collecting experiences. It came about through my falling upon an exceptionally intelligent British clerk in Brentano's in Paris. It was late in August and Europe was teetering on the edge of war. I was bound for Morocco and had to catch a train to Marseilles. In the taxi I recollected, to my dismay, that I had no books to beguile my journey. Directing the driver to stop at Brentano's I rushed into that bookstore. 'I want something in the style of James Joyce,' I said, 'and I have to have it in a hurry.' Without any hesitation my guardian angel, in the person of this anonymous clerk, reached for the stacks and handed me: Miller's *Tropic of Cancer*, *Black Spring* and *Max*, together with Lawrence Durrell's *Black Book*. I had never heard of either writer and few others had; indeed I am constantly meeting Americans today who stare blankly when I mention Miller.

I had only to read a few pages of Miller to be convinced that here was a bold new spirit, venturing to speak his mind in defiance of the cant of our century. I must confess that Durrell impressed me less although I have since come to modify my opinion of him after reading *Justine* and *Balthazar*. I was examining Durrell's *Black*

Book the other day and found it to have been a first. So also was Miller's *Black Spring* and *Max*. The lot probably cost me less than a pound. As soon as I got back to New York in September I began picking up all the Millers I could find. They included his *Miscellanea,* published by Bern Porter in only 500 copies, each with an original holograph of Miller. Mine was a postcard to Bern Porter:

Bern: I hope you at least made an exception in Schnelloch's case and sent him a *free* copy of *Semblance!* The fact that he can order copies from you proves nothing. You seem to regard a friend as one who does something *for you.* Wouldn't it be better to look upon him first and foremost as one to whom *you do something for?* Henry Miller.

Nothing could be more characteristic of Miller than the thought expressed in this card. Alfred Perlès, in his superb biography of Miller, was a thousand times right when he described him as "a genuine saint." This must have perplexed a great many people but it is a thoroughly sound appreciation. Miller's sainthood is one of his titles to fame; it may be that he is the only genuine saint to be found in the United States. In case you are incredulous read his *A Devil in Paradise.*

Some will object, "but what about his pornography"? In Edwin Corle's masterly introduction to Miller's *The Smile at the Foot of the Ladder,* Corle properly remarks that any obscenity to be found in the *Tropics* and in one or two other works of Miller, is a reflection of the obscenity in the minds of Miller's readers rather than in Miller's own. I agree wholeheartedly with Corle that Miller "is a thoroughly respectable writer." I have been reading the classics of world literature since my childhood; there are but two other writers comparable to him in the sense he gives of absolute genuineness: Shakespeare and Chekhov. One finds it also in Casanova but perhaps not as consistently.

It is a bitter commentary on the state of the world that the United States, which permits the diffusion of comic books which traduce all that is noble in man, and permits the export of certain moving pictures which are a disgrace both to the United States and to humanity, should still ban some of Miller's works. When I was Ambassador to Ethiopia and was appealed to by certain American motion picture interests to induce that government to lift the ban on gangster films I called on the authorities, showed them the letter and remarked: "I have come not to ask you to lift the ban but to congratulate you on its maintenance." As a result of the American official attitude towards Miller the tendency has been to give foreigners not acquainted with his work a wholly false and distorted opinion of him. Some time ago I invited a group of French and other residents in Nice, interested in literature, to a symposium on Miller. Most of them came to scoff. I read for the particular benefit of my French guests that moving tribute to France in the *Air-Conditioned Nightmare,* recounting Miller's visit to Sarlat and his reflections on France in that country's darkest hour after Miller's return to America. There was hardly a dry eye when I had finished. A French professor, author of many books, remarked, 'This is a revelation to me. I had no faintest notion of Miller's depth and power.' It is a pity but few do.

The *Air-Conditioned Nightmare* is one of my favourites. I especially cherish it not only for his tribute to France but also for his eloquent testimony regarding my other country, the South. Miller, a product of Brooklyn, has written in his chapter on "The Southland" one of the keenest appreciations of the South ever written and that is saying a great deal. I am tempted to quote pages but I must limit myself to a few lines:

The Southerner has a different rhythm, a different attitude towards life. Nothing will convince him that he was wrong; at bottom he has a supreme contempt for the men of the North. He has his own set of idols – warriors, statesmen, men of letters – whose fame and glory no defeat has ever dimmed. . . . This world of the South corresponds more nearly to the dream life which the poet imagines than do other sections of the country. Little by little this dream world is being penetrated and poisoned by the spirit of the North. . . . Amidst the embers of the past the Southerner treads his defiant way. Compared to the men of the North he is a charming, gracious, courteous, dignified, civilized being. . . . It is all over now. A new South is being born. The old South was ploughed under. But the ashes are still warm.

Only a Northerner of supremely sensitive perceptions, and one at the same time a poet, could have looked into the soul of the South and have written of it as Miller has done.

I am often asked what one should read of Miller. His *Tropics* should only be read by those who are looking in Miller for something other than dirt. His description of the telegraph company and its messengers in *Capricorn* rises to heights unsurpassed in American literature. "Via Dieppe-Newhaven" in *Max* is to be commended particularly to British readers. It is hilariously amusing and yet, with most of Miller, there is an undertone of profound sadness. Read the *Colossus of Maroussi* and you will be tempted to take the first boat for Greece. Don't expect to be instructed about that country but read it for what it reveals of Miller's intense spirituality. It is a paean in praise of the Greek spirit in which no obscene word or thought obtrudes.

It was my singular good fortune to have discovered Miller at a comparatively early date. Assigned to Tangier in 1941 and anxious to obtain the *Tropic of Capricorn* I wrote to a bookstore in Paris on a hunch for a copy. When I received a first edition at a cost of a few shillings I ordered four more copies which were subsequently distributed to friends. I continued to pursue the collection of Miller's works unremittingly before he had become famous. After I had established communication with him in 1947 I enlisted his own co-operation in helping to supply me with what I lacked. During these last years he has been most faithful in sending me or having sent to me by his publishers a copy of each of his works as they appear, most often with a dedication. I have been favoured also by friendly bookdealers: M. Bottin in Nice turned up for me not only a first edition of *Hamlet* but the *rarissime* Booster Broadside No. I, *Money and How it Gets That Way*. How it found its way to Nice will always be a mystery. In addition to a practically complete collection of Miller's works, I also have a few of his typescripts, as well as some bibliographical notes which he kindly sent me. I must have also forty or fifty letters from him, for the most part in longhand. I finally decided that it was too much of an imposition on his time to expect him to continue to write me and I wrote and abjured him to stop. When I was in Japan in 1956 I wrote him, stating that I would have a few hours in San Francisco on my arrival there during which I might make him a hurried visit to Big Sur. His reply was quite characteristic. In substance it was: 'We have never met and we need more than a couple of hours together. Let's wait until we can have a meeting at leisure.' I replied and told him he could not have paid our friendship a compliment which meant more to me.

I have a fairly valuable collection of books. If I were told I would have to leave my flat in a hurry and would have to rely for the rest of my life on those books which I might contrive to take with me I would not hesitate. They would be my Everyman Shakespeare, thirteen pocket volumes of Chekhov's short stories, Casanova's *Memoirs* and as much of Miller as I could salvage. I could then face any disaster with equanimity.

Henry Miller Collection, Walter Hines Page Library Randolph-Macon College, Ashland, Virginia

Books and Brochures by Henry Miller

BLACK SPRING. Paris: Obelisk Press, 338, Rue Saint-Honoré, [June, 1936]. 11–267 p. 19cm.
First edition.

SCENARIO (A FILM WITH SOUND). Paris: Obelisk Press, 1937. 9–39, [1] p., double front. 26cm.
This copy is No. 24 of 200 copies in this edition.
First edition.

MONEY AND HOW IT GETS THAT WAY. Paris: Booster Publications, 18 Villa Seurat, [1938]. 9–64 p. 18½cm.
"Booster Broadside No. 1."
First edition.
Inscribed: "To J. Rives Childs – owner of one of the few copies ever printed. How many, I don't remember. Nor where we got the funds to print it. What a delightful past! Henry Miller 2/4/61 [i.e., April 2, 1961]."

TROPIC OF CANCER. Paris: Obelisk Press, 16, Place Vendôme, [June, 1938]. 7–317, [1] p. 18½cm.
Fourth printing.
Inscribed: "What a day! Easter 1961 – Nice. I feel completely drunk with voyaging. Henry Miller."

MAX AND THE WHITE PHAGOCYTES. Paris: Obelisk Press, 16, Place Vendôme, [Sept., 1938]. 12–324 p. 21cm.
First edition.

BLACK SPRING. Paris: Obelisk Press, 16, Place Vendôme, [1938]. 11–269 p. 18½cm.
"Reprinted – Oct., 1938."

TROPIC OF CAPRICORN. Paris: Obelisk Press, 16, Place Vendôme, [Feb., 1939]. 11–367 p. 19cm.

First edition.

Inscribed: "Signed with great affection and admiration for J. Rives Childs Easter Sunday 2/4/61 [i.e., April 2]."

HAMLET. [Volume I.] Santurce, Puerto Rico: Carrefour, [1939]. 9–229, [1] p. 18½cm.
> Printed by the St. Catherine Press, Bruges, Belgium.
> At head of title: Henry Miller – Michael Fraenkel.
> First edition.

THE WORLD OF SEX. Printed by J[ohn] H[enry] N[ash] For Friends of Henry Miller, [1940]. 5–88 p. 25½cm.
> 1000 copies printed.

HAMLET. [Volume II.] New York: Carrefour, [May, 1941]. 465 p. 19½cm.
> At head of title: Henry Miller – Michael Fraenkel.
> Limited to 25 signed copies of which this is No. 8.
> Printed in Mexico.
> First edition.

THE COLOSSUS OF MAROUSSI. San Francisco: Colt Press, [1941]. [3]–244 p. 24cm.
> First edition.

THE WISDOM OF THE HEART. Norfolk, Conn.: New Directions, [1941]. 256 p. 22cm.
> First edition.

HAMLET. [Volume I.] New York: Carrefour, [July, 1943]. 9–392 p. 19cm.
> At head of title: Henry Miller – Michael Franckel.
> Printed in Mexico.
> Second edition.

SUNDAY AFTER THE WAR. Norfolk, Conn.: New Directions, [1944]. 9–300 p. 22cm.
> First edition.

MURDER THE MURDERER: AN EXCURUS [sic] ON WAR

FROM "THE AIR-CONDITIONED NIGHTMARE." Big Sur, [Calif.]: [Bern Porter], 1944. 70 p. 20½cm.
> First edition.

THE PLIGHT OF THE CREATIVE ARTIST IN THE UNITED STATES OF AMERICA. [Houlton, Me.: Bern Porter, 25 South Street, 1944.] [3]–38 p., illus. 21cm.
> This is copy No. 471.
> First edition.

SEMBLANCE OF A DEVOTED PAST. Berkeley, [Calif.]: Bern Porter, [Nov., 1944]. 61, [1] p., front. illus. 31cm.
> Selected letters to Emil Schnellock.
> 1150 copies printed.
> Printed by the Van Vechten Press, Metuchen, N.J.
> First edition.

HENRY MILLER MISCELLANEA. [Berkeley, Calif.]: Bern Porter, June, 1945. [x], 41 p., illus. 21cm.
> Contains original holograph postcard by Henry Miller.
> This is copy No. 67 of 500 copies printed.
> Printed by the Greenwood Press, San Mateo, Calif.
> First edition.

OBSCENITY AND THE LAW OF REFLECTION. Yonkers, N.Y.: [Oscar Baradinsky at the Alicat Book Shop], 1945. 24 p., port. 21cm.
> 750 copies offered for sale.
> First edition as separate publication.

THE AMAZING AND INVARIABLE BEAUFORD DELANEY. Yonkers, N.Y.: Alicat Book Shop, 1945. 23, [1] p., illus. 23cm.
> 750 copies offered for sale.
> First edition as separate publication.

ALLER RETOUR NEW YORK. [U.S.A.]: Printed for Private Circulation only, 1945. 7–89 p. 23½cm.
> This edition . . . limited to five hundred copies of which this is copy No. 71.
> Second edition.

WHY ABSTRACT? [New York]: New Directions, [1945]. 7–100 p. 24½cm.

Essays by Hilaire Hiler, Henry Miller, and William Saroyan.

First edition.

THE AIR-CONDITIONED NIGHTMARE. [New York]: A New Directions Book, 1945. 7–292 p. 22cm.

First edition.

Inscribed: "For J. Rives Childs, who seems to think this one of my best – perhaps one of the very few to think so. What a great great pleasure to come face to face with him at last – in a civilized world. Henry Miller Nice Easter Sunday 1961."

TROPIQUE DU CANCER. [Paris]: Éditions Denoël, [1945]. 348 p. 20cm.

Tr. by Paul Rivert; preface by Henri Fluchère.

Copy No. 443 of 1000.

MAURIZIUS FOREVER. San Francisco: Colt Press, March, 1946. 5–77, [1] p. 25cm.

500 copies printed.

Printed at the Grabhorn Press, San Francisco.

The illustrations are from original drawings and watercolors by the author.

First edition.

MONEY AND HOW IT GETS THAT WAY. [Berkeley, Calif.]: Bern Porter, 1946. 46 p., illus. 24cm.

Second edition.

Inscribed: "For J. Rives Childs. Written on a wager with Fraenkel – Paris! A burlesque-satire. Henry Miller 5/10/50."

TROPIQUE DU CAPRICORNE. Paris: Éditions du Chêne, [1946]. 505 p. 18½cm.

Tr. by Jean-Claude Lefaure.

First French edition.

PATCHEN: MAN OF ANGER AND LIGHT. [New York: Padell, 1947.] 32 p. 24cm.

Includes: A Letter to God, by Kenneth Patchen, pp. 23–32.
First edition.

OF, BY AND ABOUT HENRY MILLER. Yonkers, N.Y.: Printed by L. Porgie for The Alicat Bookshop Press, June, 1947. 43 p., ports. 31cm.
750 copies . . . for sale.
First edition.
Inscribed: "For J. Rives Childs – from Henry Miller 5/15/50."

REMEMBER TO REMEMBER. [New York]: A New Directions Book, [1947]. v–xxxvii, 3–427 p. 22cm.
First edition.

MAX ET LES PHAGOCYTES. [Paris]: Éditions du Chêne, [1947]. 360 p. 18½cm.
Tr. by Jean-Claude Lefaure.
Copy No. 249 of 325.

THE SMILE AT THE FOOT OF THE LADDER. New York: Duell, Sloan and Pearce, [1948]. 124 p., illus., facsim. 24cm.
First edition.
Inscribed: "To J. Rives Childs – who tells me he got this copy in Jidda, Arabia – one of the places I have dreamed about. (Here are the three: Mecca, Lhassa and Timbuctoo!) Henry Miller 2/4/61 [i.e., April 2]."

SEXUS. Paris: Obelisk Press, [1949]. 2 vol. 19½cm.
Book One of *The Rosy Crucifixion*.
This edition . . . limited to 3000 copies of which this is No. 58.
First edition.

BEZALEL SCHATZ. San Francisco: San Francisco Museum of Art, 1949. 15 unnumb. p. 27cm.
San Francisco Museum of Art Exhibition of Oil Paintings August 16 through September 11, 1949.
Foreword by Henry Miller.

500 copies printed.
Printed by the Superior Press, Berkeley, Calif.
First edition.
Inscribed: "For J. Rives Childs – the 'friend' who
knows the Yemenites. Henry Miller. 5/10/50."

THE WATERS REGLITTERIZED. [San Jose, Calif.]: John
Kidis, 1950. [47] p., plates, port. 23cm.
Limited to 1,000 copies of which this copy is No.
208.
First edition.
Inscribed: "For J. Rives Childs – for his collection.
Ever warmly, Henry Miller 12/30/50."

BLAISE CENDRARS. [Paris]: Denoël, [1951]. 71, [1] p.,
port. 28½cm.
Tr. by François Villié.
This copy is No. 846.
First edition as separate publication.

THE BOOKS IN MY LIFE. [Norfolk, Conn.]: New Direc-
tions, [1952]. 323 p. 22cm.
Printed in the Republic of Ireland.
First edition.
Inscribed: "For J. Rives Childs in far off Ethiopia –
lucky man! Henry Miller 10/4/52."

PLEXUS. Paris: Olympia Press, [1953]. 2 vols. 18½cm.
Book Two of *The Rosy Crucifixion*.
First edition in English.
This edition . . . limited to 2000 copies of which
this is no. 828.

SOUVENIR SOUVENIRS. [Paris]: Gallimard, [1953]. 347 p.
20½cm.
Tr. by André Michel.
Seventh edition.

DAS LÄCHELN AM FUSSE DER LEITER. Vienna-Munich:
Donau Verlag, [1954]. 59 p. 18½cm.
Illustrations by Gergard Swoboda.

NIGHTS OF LOVE AND LAUGHTER. [New York]: New American Library, [Nov., 1955]. 143 p. 18cm.
    A Signet book.
    First printing.

THE TIME OF THE ASSASSINS: A STUDY OF RIMBAUD. London: Neville Spearman, [1956]. xi, 163 p. 20cm.
    First English edition.

QUIET DAYS IN CLICHY. Paris: Olympia Press, 8, Rue de Nesle, [July], 1956. 7–171 p., illus., photos. 17½cm.
    "First and original edition."
    Inscribed: "For J. Rives Childs who has made me drunk with cities and places – just fabulous! I envy you. Henry Miller 2/4/61 [i.e., April 2]."

A DEVIL IN PARADISE. [New York]: New American Library, [1956]. 5–128 p. 18cm.
    A Signet book.
    First printing, July, 1956.
    Inscribed: "For J. Rives Childs from his friend Henry Miller 8/11/56."

UN DIABLE AU PARADIS. Paris: Buchet-Chastel, [1956]. 189 p. 18½cm.
    Tr. by Alex Grall.

BIG SUR AND THE ORANGES OF HIERONYMUS BOSCH. [New York]: A New Directions Book, [1957]. x, 404 p., illus. 21cm.
    First edition.
    Inscribed: "For J. Rives Childs warmly. Henry Miller 5/30/57."

THE WORLD OF SEX. Rev. ed. Paris: Olympia Press, 8, Rue de Nesle, [May], 1957. 5–132 p. 17½cm.
    Second edition.

LES LIVRES DE MA VIE. Paris: Gallimard, [1957]. 430 p. 20½cm.
    Tr. by Jean Rosenthal.
    First French edition.

Inscribed: "See appendix for list of 'books read' Henry Miller."

PORNOGRAPHY AND OBSCENITY. Michigan City, Ind.: Fridtjof-Karla Publications, Sycamore Hollow, Old Moon Road, 1958. vi, 54 p., ports. 30½cm.
> Two essays by D. H. Lawrence and Henry Miller.
> First edition as separate publication.

THE RED NOTEBOOK. [Highlands, N.C.: Jonathan Williams, 1958.] 86 p., illus., ports., facsim. 20½cm.
> First edition.
> Inscribed: "For J. Rives Childs from his friend Henry Miller 1/7/59."

REUNION IN BARCELONA. [Northwood, Middlesex]: Scorpion Press, 1959. 38 p. 22cm.
> This first edition in English . . . is limited to 500 copies of which this is No. 80.

THE INTIMATE HENRY MILLER. [New York]: New American Library, [1959]. xii, 13-191 p., illus., ports. 18cm.
> Introduction by Lawrence Clark Powell.
> First printing, April, 1959.

THE HENRY MILLER READER. Edited by Lawrence Durrell. [Norfolk, Conn.]: New Directions, [1959]. xvi, [1], 3-397 p. 21½cm.
> Includes chronology and bibliography.
> First edition.

TO PAINT IS TO LOVE AGAIN. Alhambra, Calif.: Cambria Books, [1960]. 7-64 p., 14 color plates. 20cm.
> Paperbound.
> First edition.

NEXUS. [Volume 1.] Paris: Obelisk Press, [June, 1960]. [7]-378 p. 18cm.
> First edition.

EIN WEIHNACHTSABEND IN DER VILLA SEURAT. [Hamburg]: Rowohlt, [Dec.], 1960. 23, [1] p., illus., facsim. 19cm.

A translation of part of chapter "Remember to Remember" in book of same name.

First edition as separate publication.

Inscribed: "Dear Ambassador! Just read your touching text in 'The Private Library' (thanks to Ben Grauer). Here I am in Germany – since 3 months. Soon to Paris, then South. Hope to see you in Nice before winter is over. The Tropics are coming out shortly – in Hebrew, in Italian, in Spanish, in Dutch – and in America by the Grove Press, N.Y. (But keep this under your hat, please!) Warm greetings! Henry Miller (Reinbek) 2/6/61."

THE AIR-CONDITIONED NIGHTMARE. [New York: Avon, n.d.] 255 p. 18cm.
Paperbound.

TROPIC OF CANCER. New York: Grove Press, [1961]. xxxiii, 318 p. 22cm.
Introduction by Karl Shapiro: "The Greatest Living Author."
First printing of this edition.

TROPIC OF CANCER. New York: Grove Press, 1961. xxxi, 287 p. 17½cm.
With "The Greatest Living Author," introductory essay by Karl Shapiro, which first appeared in *Two Cities*, Dec. 15, 1959.
First Black Cat edition.

THE COSMOLOGICAL EYE. [Norfolk, Conn.]: New Directions, [1961? (°1939)]. 371 p. 21cm.

HENRY MILLER: WATERCOLORS, DRAWINGS, AND HIS ESSAY THE ANGEL IS MY WATERMARK! New York: Harry N. Abrams, [1962]. 39 p., illus., 12 col. plates, ports. 33cm.
First edition.

STAND STILL LIKE THE HUMMING BIRD. [Norfolk, Conn.]: A New Directions Book, [1962]. x, [1], 194 p. 22cm.
First edition.

TROPIC OF CAPRICORN. New York: Grove Press, [1962]. 9–348 p. 22cm.
    First printing of this edition.

JUST WILD ABOUT HARRY: A MELO-MELO IN SEVEN SCENES. [Norfolk, Conn.]: New Directions, [1963]. 7–127 p. 21cm.
    First edition.

LAWRENCE DURRELL [and] HENRY MILLER: A PRIVATE CORRESPONDENCE. Edited by George Wickes. New York: E. P. Dutton & Co., 1963. xv, 3–400 p., ports. 22cm.
    First edition.

HENRY MILLER ON WRITING. Selected by Thomas H. Moore from the published and unpublished works of Henry Miller. [Norfolk, Conn.]: New Directions, [1964]. vi, 216 p., facsim. 21cm.
    Paperbound.
    First edition, second printing.

LETTERS TO ANAÏS NIN. Edited and with an introduction by Gunther Stahlmann. New York: G. P. Putnam's Sons, [1965]. xxvi, 356 p., facsim. 22cm.
    First edition.

SELECTED PROSE. [London]: Macgibbon & Kee, 1965. 2 vols. 22½cm.

ORDER AND CHAOS CHEZ HANS REICHEL. New Orleans: Loujon Press, [1966]. 7–87, [4] p., illus., facsim. 25½cm.
    Introduction by Lawrence Durrell.
    Limited first edition.

Contributions to Books, Periodicals,
and Book Reviews by Henry Miller

"II – Soirée in Hollywood," *Horizon*, VII, No. 38 (Feb., 1943), [133]–41.
    Fragment from THE AIR-CONDITIONED NIGHTMARE.

"Knud Merrill: A Holiday in Paint," *Circle Magazine* [No. 6 (1945)].
　　Offprint.

"The Letter to Lafayette." In THE ATLANTIC ANTHOLOGY. Ed. Nicholas Moore and Douglas Newton. London: Fortune Press, 1945.

"Shadowy Monomania." In NEW ROAD: DIRECTIONS IN EUROPEAN ART AND LETTERS. Ed. Fred Marnau. London: Grey Walls Press, 1945.

Review of *Quest,* by George Dibbern, *Circle Magazine,* VII–VIII (1946), 1–6.
　　Offprint.

"Into the Night Life." Los Angeles: George Yamada, n.d. 14 unnumb. 1. 28cm.
　　Publicity brochure.

"Books Tangent to Circle," *Circle Magazine,* n.d.
　　Offprint.
　　Reviews of MEN GOD FORGOT, by Albert Cossery, LIFE AFTER DEATH, by G. T. Fechner, and QUEST, by George Dibbern.

"The Red Herring and the Diamond-Backed Terrapin." Introduction to ART IN CINEMA. Ed. Frank Stauffacher. [San Francisco]: Art in Cinema Society [and] San Francisco Museum of Art, 1947.

Preface to Milton Mezzrow and Bernard Wolfe, LA RAGE DE VIVRE. Tr. Marcel Duhamel and Madelaine Gautier. Paris: Éditions Corrêa, [1950].
　　LA RAGE DE VIVRE is a translation of REALLY THE BLUES.

"From a Book about Books," *Survival,* No. 1 (Autumn, 1950), 10–26.

"Reflections on Writing." In THE CREATIVE PROCESS: A SYMPOSIUM. Ed. Brewster Ghiselin. New York: New American Library, 1952.

"Un Caillou blanc," *Prospectus,* VI–VII (Jan.–Feb., 1954), 2–8.

> Article on the re-issue of Haniel Long's translation of Cabeza de Vaca.

"Third Fragment from 'The Rosy Crucifixion.'" In Stories for Tonight. New York: Avon Publications, 1955.

"When I Reach for My Revolver." In *7 Arts,* No. 3. Ed. Fernando Puma. Indian Hills, Colo.: Falcon's Wing Press, 1955.

"Literature as a Dead Duck," *London Magazine,* III, No. 3 (March, 1956), 43–47.

[Letters to David D. Burliuk], *Color and Rhyme,* No. 31 (1956), 33 [letter dated 11/4/55]; *ibid.,* No. 40 (Summer, 1959), n.p. [letter dated Dec. 8th 1954].

"The Hour of Man," *Chicago Review,* X, No. 3 (Autumn-Winter, 1956), 1–8.

> Offprint.

Review of The Third Eye, by T. Lobsang Rampa. 1957.

> Offprint used as publicity release.

"A Great Writer Talks about Astrology." In Sidney Omarr, *1958* Guidebook to Astrology. Los Angeles, Calif.: Trend Books, 1958. 24cm.

> Correction by Miller in ink on p. 127.

"Children of the Earth," *Prairie Schooner,* XXXII, No. 3 (Fall, 1958), 161–69.

"Let the Children Play with the Lock," *Orgonomic Functionalism,* V, No. 6 (Nov., 1958), 361–64.

"The Durrell of the Black Book Days," *Two Cities,* No. 1 (April, 1959), 3–10.

"Children of the Earth," *London Magazine,* VI, No. 7 (July, 1959), 13–21.

"Defense of the Freedom to Read," *Two Cities,* No. 2 (July 15, 1959), 16–22.

"Jours heureux à Die," *Relâche*, Spring, 1960, pp. 6–12.
    Letter to Francis Druart, tr. Albert Maillet.

"Lime Twigs and Treachery," *Between Worlds*, I, No. 1
    (Summer, 1960), 33–39.

"Ionesco's Soprano Punched a Time Clock," *Between
    Worlds*, I, No. 1 (Summer, 1960), 99–112.

"From the World of Sex," *Evergreen Review*, V, No. 17
    (March–April, 1961), 20–31.

"Woman throughout the Ages." Introduction to THE IM-
    AGE OF WOMAN: WOMEN IN SCULPTURE FROM PRE-
    HISTORIC TIMES TO THE PRESENT DAY. Concept and
    photography by Andreas Feininger. Text and cap-
    tions by J. Bon. London: Thames and Hudson, 1961.

[Letters to Walter Lowenfels], ed. Jon Edgar Webb, *The
    Outsider* (New Orleans, La.), I, Nos. 1–3 (Fall, 1961;
    Summer, 1962; Spring, 1963).
    Letters were written in the 1930's.

"Joseph Delteil," *Aylesford Review*, IV, No. 7 (Summer,
    1962), [247]–50.
    On pp. 276–77 of this issue there is another article
    by Miller on Joseph Delteil in French, written orig-
    inally in the autumn of 1956.

"Why I Wrote 'Tropic of Cancer,'" *Miami Herald*,
    March 3, 1963.
    Written for the Los Angeles *Times*.

Preface to H. E. Bates, SEVEN BY FIVE. London: Michael
    Joseph, 1963.

"Revolt in the Desert," *Cavalier*, XV, No. 139 (Jan.,
    1965), [30–32].

Manuscripts by Henry Miller

Letters to J. Rives Childs, July 26, 1957 – December 13,
    1965. 40 letters and 11 postal cards.

A few letters are typewritten; the majority are holograph.

The collection also includes copies of 32 of Childs's letters to Henry Miller written during the same period.

"Literature as a Dead Duck." [1]–6 p. 28cm.
 Typescript on yellow and green second sheets.
 Numerous corrections and rewritings of text in Miller's handwriting in pencil and in ink; last page almost completely holograph.
 Title "Literature as a Dead Duck" handwritten in ink, struck through with pencil; written above this "When I Reach for My Revolver" – Henry Miller. Text appears, however, in *London Magazine* (March, 1956) under title "Literature as a Dead Duck."

"Mara-Marignan." [1]–45 p. 28cm.
 Carbon copy on onionskin of a typescript. Miller's signature and address are written in ink on first sheet and a few ink corrections made in text.

"My Life as an Echo (with apologies to Moishe Nadir)." 8 p. 28cm.
 Carbon copy of typescript.

"Stand Still Like the Humming Bird!" [1]–15 p. 28cm.
 Photocopy of a typescript.
 Original typescript was marked with Miller's handwritten corrections. Big Sur, California. Dec. 20th, 1959.

"Suggestions for Corrections in Translation of Text in *Synthèses* (Juin 1954) of 'Quand Je Saisis Mon Revolver.'" [1]–5 p. 28cm.
 Carbon copy of typescript on orange second sheets.

"The Waters Reglitterized." 2 l [1]–34 p. 28cm.
 Carbon copy of typescript.

"When I Reach for My Revolver." [1]–21 p. 28cm.

    Carbon copy of typescript on blue, yellow, and orange second sheets.

    Cover sheet with note in Miller's handwriting: "appeared in Synthèses (Belgium) in French   Chicago Review has copy *Puma* – to appear in pocketbook soon (11/55)"

Books and Brochures about Henry Miller

THE HAPPY ROCK: A BOOK ABOUT HENRY MILLER. [Berkeley, Calif.: Bern Porter, 1945.] 157 p., illus., facsims. 27cm.

    Essays by over 25 contributors, including Lawrence Durrell, Alfred Perlès, Wallace Fowlie.

    Printed by the Packard Press, Berkeley, Calif.

    Inscribed: "For J. Rives Childs from the 'rock' hisself! Henry Miller 10/16/56."

Porter, Bern[ard H.]. HENRY MILLER: A CHRONOLOGY AND BIBLIOGRAPHY. [Berkeley, Calif.: The author, May, 1945.] 36 p. 23cm.

    Of 500 numbered copies, this is copy no. 139.

    Printed by the Waverly Press, Baltimore, Md.

Fraenkel, Michael. DÉFENSE DU TROPIQUE DU CANCER: AVEC DES INÉDITS DE MILLER. Paris: Variété, 108, Avenue du Maine, [June, 1947]. 13–93 p. 19½cm.

    Of 3,051 copies, this copy is no. 1693.

HENRY MILLER; OU, LES MAUVAISES FRÉQUENTATIONS. *La Tour de Feu* (Paris), No. 47 (Autumn, 1955). [138] p. 22½cm.

Perlès, Alfred. MY FRIEND HENRY MILLER. London: Neville Spearman, [1955]. 242 p., port. 22cm.

    Preface by Henry Miller.

ART AND OUTRAGE: A CORRESPONDENCE ABOUT HENRY MILLER BETWEEN ALFRED PERLÈS AND LAWRENCE

Durrell. (With an intermission by Henry Miller.) London: Putnam, 1959. 7–63 p., port. 22cm.

Perlès, Alfred. Reunion in Big Sur: A Letter to Henry Miller in Reply to His *Reunion in Barcelona.* [Northwood, Middlesex, Eng.]: Scorpion Press, 1959. 7–37 p. 22cm.

Omarr, Sydney. Henry Miller: His World of Urania. Hollywood, Calif.: 9th House Publishing Company, 1960. 108 p., illus. 22cm.
> Foreword by Henry Miller.
> Printed by Villiers Publications Ltd., London.

Baxter, Annette Kar. Henry Miller, Expatriate. [Pittsburgh]: University of Pittsburgh Press, [1961]. 201 p. 19cm.

Moore, Thomas Hamilton. Bibliography of Henry Miller. Minneapolis: Henry Miller Literary Society, [1961]. 32 p., port., facsims. 23cm.

Schmiele, Walter. Henry Miller in Selbstzengnissen und Bildokumenten. [Reinbek bei Hamburg]: Rowohlt, [1961]. 177 p. 19cm.
> Inscribed: "Dear friend – Here's another to add to your ever-growing collection. Henry Miller (Reinbek) 22/8/61."

White, Emil, ed. Henry Miller: Between Heaven and Hell. Big Sur, Calif.: Big Sur Publications, 1961. 102 p., illus. 21½cm.

The International Henry Miller Letter (Nijmegen, Netherlands), Nos. 1–6 (June, 1961–April, 1964). Ed. Henk van Gelre.

Perlès, Alfred. My Friend Henry Miller. New York: Belmont Books, 1962. lx, 189 p. 17½cm.
> With preface by Miller written especially for this edition.

Widmer, Kingsley. Henry Miller. New York: Twayne Publishers, [1963]. 13–192 p. 21cm.

Wickes, George, ed. HENRY MILLER AND THE CRITICS. Carbondale, [Ill.]: Southern Illinois University Press, [1964]. xviii, 194 p. 21½cm.

Slotnikoff, Will. THE FIRST TIME I LIVE. Washington: Manchester Lane Editions, [1966]. 7–238 p. 18½cm.
First printing.
"Includes an exchange of letters with Henry Miller on what might well serve to illustrate 'The Creative Process in Action.'"

Gordon, William A. THE MIND AND ART OF HENRY MILLER. [Baton Rouge]: Louisiana State University Press, [1967]. vi–xxxii, 3–232 p. 23cm.
Foreword by Lawrence Durrell.
First edition.

Reviews of Miller's Books and Other Periodical Articles about Miller

Durrell, Lawrence. "Studies in Genius VIII – Henry Miller," *Horizon*, XX, No. 115 (July, 1949), 45–61.

Haan, J. den. "A Dream of a Book," *Kroniek van Kunst en Kultuur* (Amsterdam, Netherlands), Dec., 1949.
Offprint.
Review of INTO THE NIGHT LIFE.

Steiner, Rudolph. "Henry Miller – a Debt," *Span*, No. 2.
Inscribed: "letter soon! H.M."

Read, Herbert. "Herbert Read on Henry Miller," *New English Weekly*, n.d.
Offprint.

"Henry Miller encore une fois," *La Tour de Feu*, No. 51 (Autumn, 1956), 151–54.
Letters from Henry Miller, Claude Pelieu, Henri Chabrol, Adrian Miatlev, Frederick Tristan, and Jean-Paul Samson in response to special issue on Miller.

Read, Herbert. In *New Statesman,* March 29, 1958. Offprint.
Review of Big Sur and the Oranges of Hierony-mus Bosch.

Morice-Kerne. "La Lecture heureuse," *L'École mater-nelle française,* April, 1958, pp. 4–6+.

National Institute of Arts and Letters. *Proceedings,* 2d Ser., No. 8 (1958).
Report of induction of newly elected members including Henry Miller.

Powell, Lawrence Clark. "The Miller of Big Sur." In his Books in My Baggage. Cleveland: World Publishing Company, 1959.

Henry Miller Literary Society, Minneapolis, Minn. *Newsletter,* Nos. 1–13 (1959–Nov., 1964).

Shapiro, Karl. "The Greatest Living Author," *Two Cities,* No. 3 (Dec. 15, 1959), 25–44.

Weber, Jean-Paul. "Tout le monde est anarchiste," *L'Express* (Paris), Feb. 11, 1960.
Review of Nexus.

Thibaut, Philippe. "Un Avatar de Rimbaud: Henry Miller," *Relâche* (Summer, 1960), 29–31.

Trilling, Lionel. "Angels and Ministers of Grace," *The Mid-Century,* No. 31 (Oct., 1961).
Review of The Henry Miller Reader.

Bess, Donovan. "Miller's 'Tropic' on Trial," *Evergreen Review,* VI, No. 23 (March–April, 1962), 12–37.

Delteil, Joseph. "Henry Miller (Fusain)," *Aylesford Review,* IV, No. 7 (Summer, 1962), 278–80.

Norris, Hoke. " 'Cancer' in Chicago," *Evergreen Review,* VI, No. 25 (July–Aug., 1962), [40]–66.

Wickes, George. "The Art of Fiction, XXVIII: Henry Miller," *Paris Review,* VII, No. 28 (Summer-Fall, 1962), 128–39.

Roche, Denis. In *La Quinzaine littéraire,* No. 36 (Oct. 1–15, 1967), 12–13.
Review of LETTRES À ANAÏS NIN.

Clippings include reviews of Miller's books published between 1947 and 1965 in the following periodicals and newspapers:

Adelaide *Advertiser* (Australia)
Carrefour (Paris)
Figaro (Paris)
Le Monde (Paris)
New Statesman (London)
New York *Herald-Tribune* (New York and Paris editions)
New York *Times Book Review*
Newsweek
Le Nouveau Candide (Paris)
Le Patriote (Paris)
Saturday Review
Time
Times-Dispatch (Richmond)
Times Literary Supplement (London)
Times-Picayune (New Orleans)

Index

Index

The Collector's Quest

was composed, printed, and bound by the Kingsport Press, Inc., Kingsport, Tennessee. The text paper is Warren's Olde Style, and the types are Caledonia and News Gothic Bold. Design is by Edward G. Foss.